THE INCREDIBLE GUIDE

LONDON, NEW YORK, MUNICH,
MELBOURNE, and DELHI

Editor Alastair Dougall
Designer Dan Bunyan
Publishing Manager Cynthia O'Neill
Art Director Mark Richards
Production Nicola Torode
DTP Designer Jill Bunyan
Marvel Editorial Consultants Seth Lehman, Jeff Youngquist

First American Edition, 2003
03 04 05 06 07 10 9 8 7 6 5 4 3 2 1

Published in the United States by
DK Publishing, Inc.
375 Hudson Street
New York, New York 10014

DK Publishing, Inc. offers special discounts for bulk purchases for sales promotions or premiums. Specific, large-quantity needs can be met with special editions, including personalized covers, excerpts of existing guides, and corporate imprints. For more information, contact Special Markets Department, DK Publishing, Inc., 375 Hudson Street, New York, NY 10014. Fax: 800-600-9098.

Library of Congress Cataloging-in-Publication Data

DeFalco, Tom.
   The Hulk : the incredible guide / by Tom DeFalco.-- 1st American ed.
      p. cm.
   ISBN 0-7894-9260-1 (hard cover)
   1. Hulk (Comic strip) 2. Incredible Hulk (Fictitious character) I.
Title.

PN6728.H8D454 2002
741.5'973--dc21

                                        2002154785

Reproduced by Media Development and Printing Ltd., UK
Printed and bound in Italy by Mondadori

See our complete product line at
www.dk.com

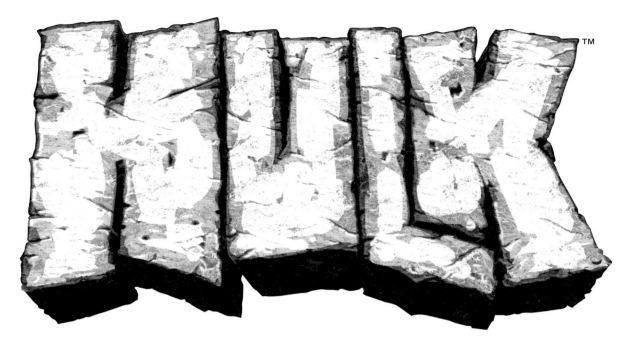

HULK™

THE INCREDIBLE GUIDE

TOM DEFALCO

DK Publishing

CONTENTS

FOREWORD

I CAN'T DENY IT. I've always loved creating titles that contained adjectives.

As evidence, I offer you The Amazing Spider-Man, The Uncanny X-Men, The Fantastic Four and—well, you get the idea.

When I first decided to call Bruce Banner's monstrous alter ego The Hulk, I knew that something was sorely lacking. He was too big and powerful for such a simple name. If ever a character needed an adjective, he was that one, for he was too incredible to merely be called The Hulk. That's when it hit me. "Incredible" was the adjective I'd been seeking. And lo, a title was born.

I'll be the first to admit that The Incredible Hulk is not your typical type of hero. Actually, it all depends on how one defines the word "hero." Let me tell you how I feel about it.

It all started with the old classic movie, *Frankenstein*, starring Boris Karloff. When I saw that movie many years ago, I thought the monster was the hero. I'll admit he was scary-looking, but he was really a good guy. He didn't want to hurt anyone until those brainless townspeople kept chasing him with their guns and torches and he finally lashed out in panic and confusion.

To tell the truth, I was on the monster's side all through the movie.

That's what first gave me the idea of creating a heroic monster, a creature who was basically good at heart but who would be continually hunted and hounded by society. The Incredible Hulk was my own personal homage to *Frankenstein*.

But another classic story influenced me, as well. Feeling that it might be difficult to give the Hulk's tales enough complexity if they consisted of nothing more than a monstrous being terrorizing the countryside for page after page, I thought about Robert Louis Stevenson's unforgettable tale *Dr. Jekyll and Mr. Hyde*.

You may recall that Dr. Jekyll was a fine, upstanding English physician who was transformed into the ugly, evil Mr. Hyde when he drank a strange potion he had concocted. The idea of a character transforming from normal to monstrous and back to normal again intrigued me.

So, enter Bruce Banner. With his inclusion, the series seemed to take on the aspect of a Greek tragedy. We had a tortured soul who never knew when he might uncontrollably change into a rampaging monster. Until a cure could be found, he would never know a minute's peace, never have the chance to lead a normal life or dare to wed the girl he loved.

But there's so much more to tell about The Incredible Hulk. To learn about the thrilling storylines and to meet the whole panoply of fantastic characters, you have the very best possible guide in the person of Tom DeFalco.

Tom, who is a close and valued friend of mine, has been a top writer and Editor-in-chief of Marvel Comics. No one is better qualified to lead you into the wondrous world that lies ahead.

May you enjoy the fabulous legend that follows as much as I did, those long, exciting years ago.

Excelsior!

Stan Lee

BRUCE BANNEr

Bruce possesses a mind so brilliant that it cannot be measured by any known intelligence test.

HE ALMOST DIED at birth and often wishes he had. Robert Bruce Banner is the only son of Brian and Rebecca Banner and he had a very unhappy childhood. Bruce's father was an atomic physicist who worked for the U.S. government. The more Brian learned about radiation, the more he feared it. He started drinking to deal with his mounting stress and began to suspect that he had been exposed to trace amounts of radiation. Fearing it had altered his genetic structure, he was horrified to learn that Rebecca was pregnant. She suffered many medical complications and Brian became convinced that his son, Bruce, was some kind of a mutant. Although Bruce seemed a normal, healthy baby, Brian was convinced he would grow up to be a monster.

Daddy Dearest
Brian's paranoia increased when Bruce began to show signs of a gifted intellect. Rebecca tried to defend her son, but Brian took his frustrations out on her and became increasingly more abusive. When she decided to leave him, Brian accidentally killed her in a fit of anger.

IN FATHER'S FOOTSTEPS
Brian Banner had an explosive temper and often lashed out at anyone who annoyed him. Young Bruce often watched in helpless horror as his father struck his mother. He prayed that one day he'd be strong enough to protect her.

REPRESSED EMOTIONS

Though still a child, Bruce tried to cover for his father during the resulting murder investigation, but Brian Banner was eventually convicted of manslaughter and sentenced to a mental institution. Bruce was sent to live with his mother's sister, Mrs. Elizabeth Drake. He was a shy and quiet child who rarely expressed any kind of emotion. The Drakes tried to get him to come out of his shell and enrolled him in a private school for gifted science students.

Bruce Banner stands 5-ft-9-in tall and weighs about 130 lb.

Problems at School

Science was the only thing that mattered to young Bruce. He devoted all his time and energy to his studies and ignored his classmates. He decided to become a doctor, but always remained fascinated with the study of radiation, the one thing that scared his father. In his spare time, Bruce began to research gamma radiation and came to believe that it could be used to cure many diseases. He also theorized that a gamma bomb could be designed to destroy property but leave the people alive.

Bruce's classmates mistook his shyness for arrogance and often made him the butt of their pranks.

A FATEFUL DECISION
Bruce, though always a little shy, made a real effort to fit in with the other students when he went to college. However, his interest in gamma radiation intensified: after two years, he dropped out of medical school and decided to become a nuclear physicist.

Dr. Bruce cannot trust anyone, not even himself.

A MAN OF MANY FACES
Hunted by the authorities, Bruce Banner has donned many disguises over the years and recently shaved his head.

Always on the Run

Ever since the accident that transformed him into the Hulk, Bruce Banner has been a man on the run. He has run from the police, the government, clandestine forces, and the beast that lives within him. Recently accused of murdering a young boy named Ricky Myers, Banner attempted to clear himself while on the run.

Haunted by the Hulk

Ever since he was a child, Bruce Banner has suffered from nightmares. A monster stalked his dreams, destroying everything in its path. After being treated by Doctor Samson, Bruce realized that this was how he had always seen his father. It is also the way he sees himself. In many ways, his relationship with the Hulk mirrors the one he had father. Bruce is trapped in a never-ending nightmare. He must contain the raging beast within or it will destroy everything he loves.

ORIGIN OF THE HULK

The Hulk is considerably taller and at least 900 lb heavier than Bruce Banner.

AFTER EARNING advanced degrees in nuclear physics, Dr. Bruce Banner worked for the U.S. Defense Department, continuing his research in gamma radiation. He began to develop a gamma or G-bomb and was assigned to a New Mexico missile base commanded by General Thaddeus "Thunderbolt" Ross. Ross assigned Igor Starsky as Banner's chief research assistant. However, Starsky's real name was Igor Drenkov and he was a Russian spy. Igor's mission was to steal Banner's secrets and prevent America from developing the G-bomb. As work on the bomb progressed, Igor grew increasingly frustrated because Dr. Banner refused to share his formulas. Sabotage delayed the bomb's underground test for a number of weeks, until General Ross lost patience and ordered Banner to start the countdown.

SECURITY BREACH

On the morning of the G-bomb's test, Dr. Banner was stationed in a concrete command bunker where he quietly rechecked his calculations. Meanwhile his staff prepped the bomb for detonation. As the final countdown began, the scientist picked up a pair of binoculars and took one last look at the test site. He was startled to see that an intruder had somehow managed to breach the base's security and enter the area.

The physical transformation from Banner to the Hulk is extremely painful, but it has grown quicker over time.

ALONE IN THE DESERT STANDS THE MOST AWESOME WEAPON EVER CREATED BY MAN—*THE INCREDIBLE G-BOMB!*

THE COLD WAR
At the time the G-bomb was developed, the U.S. was in the midst of an arms race with the former Soviet Union. Both countries had added atom and hydrogen bombs to their nuclear arsenals and were looking for even more powerful weapons. Banner believed the gamma bomb could give America a military advantage and might serve as a nuclear deterrent. He also wanted to master the power that had terrorized Brian Banner and might have driven him insane.

Panel text:
WAIT! WHAT'S *THAT?!* GOOD LORD! IT'S A BOY -- A *TEENAGER!* HE'S DRIVING INTO THE TEST AREA!

HEY! WHAT ARE YA TRYIN' TO *DO?* MAKE THEM THINK I'M *CHICKEN?*

BOMB??

COME ON, YOU FOOL! WE'VE GOT TO REACH THE PROTECTIVE TRENCH BEFORE THE BOMB GOES OFF!

THERE! YOU'RE SAFE!

AND NOW I'LL-- AHHH

THIS MESSAGE! IT IS *UNBELIEVABLE!* IN AMERICA, THERE EXISTS A CREATURE CALLED *THE HULK,* WHOSE POWER ALMOST MATCHES *MINE!*

GARGOYLE™

Betrayed by a Spy

Ordering Igor to halt the countdown, Banner attempted to warn the civilian, a teenager named Rick Jones who had entered the base on dare. Igor, however, had no intention of obeying Banner. The spy believed his boss would die in the explosion and that America couldn't complete the G-bomb without him. Though Banner reached the teenager and hurled him into a trench seconds before the bomb exploded, he was unable to save himself.

WHAT IS HAPPENING ???

ARGHH

CLICK CLICK CLICK CLICK

RADIATION BATH
Although many miles from ground zero, Bruce Banner was bathed in intense waves of gamma radiation. He somehow managed to survive due to some unknown x-factor in his genetic makeup. Rick Jones brought the unconscious scientist to the base's hospital and the two of them were placed in quarantine.

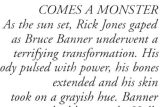

HEY! LOOK AT YOU! YOU-- *CHANGED!*

COMES A MONSTER
As the sun set, Rick Jones gaped as Bruce Banner underwent a terrifying transformation. His body pulsed with power, his bones extended and his skin took on a grayish hue. Banner had become the Hulk.

Spymaster Supreme

Igor Drenkov reported to a man who was code-named the Gargoyle. A brilliant scientific genius, the Gargoyle had been involved in an atomic accident that mutated his body and dramatically increased his intelligence. Called the Gargoyle because of his hideous appearance, he continued to pursue his career as a scientist while also forming a major Russian intelligence network for the former Soviet Union. The Gargoyle learned of the Hulk's existence and immediately arranged to kidnap him and Rick Jones. When the sun rose the following morning, the Gargoyle was shocked to find Bruce Banner instead of the monster.

DOC! YOU AIN'T GONNA *HELP* THAT CREEP, ARE YOU??!

QUIET, RICK!

NO MATTER *WHAT* HAPPENS TO ME... EVEN IF I *DIE...* SO LONG AS I COULD DIE AS-- *A MAN!*

The Hulk Strikes!

Confused by his surroundings, the Hulk ripped through the hospital's concrete wall as if it were made of cardboard. He strolled directly into the path of an onrushing jeep, crushing it on impact. An alarm was sounded and the entire base joined the hunt for the Hulk. Though he no longer remembered his past life, the Hulk returned to Banner's quarters where he discovered his assistant, Igor, rifling through his papers. He overpowered the spy, then, as the sun rose, the Hulk turned back into his former self. Dr. Bruce Banner knew that his life had changed forever.

HEY, SARGE! LOOK--AHEAD! WHAT'S *THAT?*

MEN! MORE LITTLE MEN!!

I DUNNO! BUT IF HE DOESN'T STOP, WE'LL HIT 'IM!

REDEMPTION
As soon as he learned that the Gargoyle longed to regain his human appearance, Banner used gamma radiation to cure him. The thankful man released his captives and later lost his life while trying to destroy his former Russian masters.

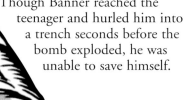

HULK'S POWERS

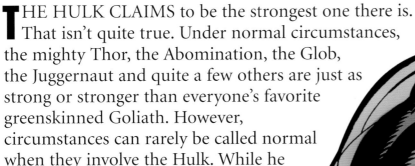

LEAPING ABILITY
The Hulk's leg muscles are so strong that he can leap nearly 3 miles in a single bound.

THE HULK CLAIMS to be the strongest one there is. That isn't quite true. Under normal circumstances, the mighty Thor, the Abomination, the Glob, the Juggernaut and quite a few others are just as strong or stronger than everyone's favorite greenskinned Goliath. However, circumstances can rarely be called normal when they involve the Hulk. While he can usually lift 70 tons without breaking a sweat, the Hulk is an inhuman engine of destruction whose strength increases in direct proportion with his anger. The longer a battle lasts, the stronger he gets and there doesn't seem to be any limit to his strength. He has been known to push aircraft carriers out of his way and to shatter mountains with his unrelenting fists.

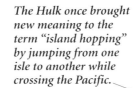

The Hulk once brought new meaning to the term "island hopping" by jumping from one isle to another while crossing the Pacific.

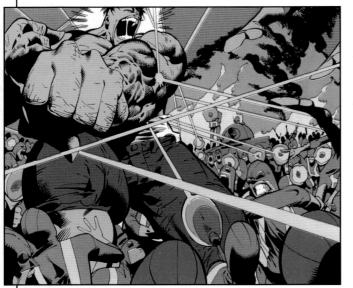

Super-Durability

The Hulk has no need to take cover when the bullets start flying. His skin resists direct hits by small arms fire, grenades, and artillery shells, as well as the high-impact blows of his usual super-powered sparring partners. He is a living armored tank who can also be exposed to almost 3,000° F without blistering and has survived temperatures as low as -190°F without freezing.

OTHER UNUSUAL TALENTS

No one has ever mistaken the Hulk for a modern day Einstein, but he does seem to have some rather amazing mental abilities. While he has no training in the mystic arts, the Hulk can perceive astral projections, which are intangible spirit forms that are invisible to most humans. He also seems highly resistant to mind control. Neither the Leader nor Zzzax has ever been able to mentally manipulate him. On the rare occasions that someone has managed to brainwash the Hulk, the effects are only temporary and he often snaps out of it on his own. He also seems to have an instinctive homing ability that enables him to return to the area in the New Mexico desert where he first became the Hulk.

Regenerative Powers

The Hulk doesn't feel pain like the rest of us. It takes something very special to injure his incredibly powerful body, and even then he doesn't care. He has the ability to heal almost any wound with lightning speed. Vector of the U-Foes once flash-fried the Hulk, burning off all his skin, but it only took a few minutes before he grew back a new layer and was completely restored. If Banner is hurt, he will be healed as soon as he transforms back into the Hulk. Old greenskin also appears to be immune to every disease on Earth, including the common cold.

THUNDERCLAPS AND TREMOR TAPS
The Hulk doesn't even need to lay a finger on his enemies to defeat them. By slamming his hands together, he can create a sonic boom with enough force to send his enemies flying. He can also generate a minor earthquake by pounding on the ground and directing the tremors toward a specific target.

The Hulk can rip up a railroad track and snap it like a bath towel, sending train cars hurtling into the sky.

SUPER-STAMINA
The Hulk never seems to tire. His endurance appears to be as unlimited as his strength. He once spent a full week swimming across the Pacific Ocean without a single pause. Time is always his greatest ally. No matter how the odds are stacked against him, he can outlast or grow strong enough to conquer any opponent.

ANGER MANAGEMENT
When Hulk wants to smash something, no force on Earth can stop him. Since the Hulk's power escalates as his anger increases, he can only be defeated if he isn't given a chance to get agitated. As Bruce Banner often warns, don't make him angry. You won't like him when he's angry.

INCARNATIONS

THE HULK WAS BORN in the heart of a nuclear explosion. Like any other newborn, he has also grown and evolved over the years. It is currently believed that Bruce Banner suffers from a physiological disease called MPD or multiple personality disorder. When Banner first became the Hulk, the creature had gray skin and could only emerge from sunset to sunrise. As Banner continued to change, the Hulk's skin took on a greenish hue and was completely green within a matter of weeks. Hoping to get rid of the monster, General Ross tricked him into entering a spaceship and blasted him into space. The Hulk was exposed to additional radiation that gave him the ability to exist during the day.

THE ROAD TO RUIN

Banner soon built a gamma-ray machine that allowed him to become the Hulk at will and still retain his own intelligence and personality. Unfortunately, the constant exposure to gamma rays took their toll. Banner's control over the monster began to slip and the Hulk grew more savage. Within a few months, the transformations started to occur on their own and Banner turned into the Hulk whenever he became agitated or angry.

A MIND AT WAR
Banner's MPD can be traced back to his traumatic childhood. Exposure to gamma rays allowed him to manifest his darker personalities as the Hulk. Each Hulk incarnation has distinctive characteristics, expressing key aspects of Banner's psyche, and they all battle for supremacy within his subconscious.

Many different versions of the Hulk have emerged from Bruce Banner over the years.

EVOLUTION OF A MONSTER
The Hulk has never stopped mutating. He has the intelligence and personality of a child on some occasions, and the genius of Bruce Banner on others. His body and posture have also changed throughout the years. The Hulk used to be 6-feet tall and now stands well over 7 feet. His weight has varied from 900 lb. to nearly 1,200.

Gray Hulk

The gray version was the first incarnation of the Hulk. He seemed to exhibit a lot of traits that embarrassed Banner, which might be one of the reasons why he could only come out at night. He was crafty, sarcastic, selfish and manipulative. In so many ways, he seemed like the typical teenager that Banner had never allowed himself to become. The Gray Hulk later took on the identity of Joe Fixit, a Las Vegas "leg breaker," and enjoyed the good life, indulging in anything that gave him pleasure.

The Gray Hulk could barely lift 70 tons, but the Savage green Hulk often carried 100 tons without strain.

I JUST WANT TO BE LEFT ALONE!

Savage Hulk

The Savage Hulk is the best known of all the Hulk's incarnations. He had a childlike mind and limited vocabulary. He usually referred to himself in the third person, and often claimed that he just wanted to be left alone. When he was a child, Banner felt powerless and unable to defend himself, so it's only fitting that the Savage Hulk may also be his most powerful incarnation.

Savage Banner

Always fearing the return of the Savage Hulk, the Professor created a psychic failsafe to prevent himself from losing his temper and going on a rampage. Whenever he became enraged, he would revert to Bruce Banner so that he would grow weaker as his anger increased.

PROFESSOR HULK
With the aid of Doc Samson, Banner merged his previous incarnations into an idealized version of the Hulk. The Professor possessed the strength of the savage Hulk, the craftiness of the gray Hulk and the intelligence of Bruce Banner, but without any of his usual fears or insecurities.

MINDLESS HULK
On more than one occasion, Bruce Banner's subconscious influence was completely removed from the Hulk, resulting in a mindless monster that only lived to survive. More animal than man, this incarnation of the Hulk stormed around in a perpetual state of anger and tried to destroy anything in its path.

RICK JONES

H E WAS DESTINED to be a loser. Orphaned at an early age, he was shuffled from orphanage to orphanage because he was a discipline problem with a bad attitude. He ran away shortly after his 13th birthday and lived on his own, supporting himself by doing menial jobs as he drifted all over the American southwest. He got his driver's license at 16 and scraped together enough money to buy an old jalopy. Rick overheard a group of teenagers discussing rumors about a new type of bomb that was soon going to be tested at a nearby missile base. Needing money, he bet the kids he could sneak onto the test site. In this way was set in motion the bizarre chain of events that would transform Bruce Banner into the Incredible Hulk.

Constant Companion

Rick Jones was at first the only one that knew Banner's secret. He felt responsible for the accident that created the Hulk and became the scientist's confidant. Rick even organized the Teen Brigade, a group of young radio enthusiasts who monitored the Hulk's activities and often helped him. Thinking that his friend was dead at one point, Rick told the world that Bruce Banner was the Hulk.

IN COMMAND
For a brief period of time, a freak accident made Rick Jones the master of the mightiest creature on Earth.

The New Captain Marvel
Rick Jones merged with an alien named Genis-Vell, son of the original Captain Marvel and one of Rick's former super-partners. Connected by a pair of Nega-Bands that allow Rick and Genis to switch atoms, the new Captain Marvel can fly and shoot energy blasts. He also possesses super-human strength and the ability to sense a threat before it occurs.

PROFESSIONAL SIDEKICK

Rick and his Teen Brigade were instrumental in the creation of the Avengers. After the Hulk quit, Rick remained with the fledgling super-team and was given honorary membership. He briefly became Captain America's partner, but later returned to the Hulk. After years of partnering with various super heroes, Rick met and married Marlo Chandler, who had once dated the Hulk. Though recently separated, Rick and Marlo still love each other and hope to get back together.

HULK FRIENDS

IT'S HARD TO BELIEVE that a big green monster with an explosive temper could have many friends, but the Hulk would surprise you. In the course of his travels, his good deeds have won the respect and loyalty of quite a few people. The first to befriend the greenskinned giant was an unnamed European scientist who was being held prisoner in the former Soviet Union. He sacrificed his life to save the Hulk. The Hulk later made friends with Mogol, a robot with super-strength that had been created by Tyrannus. At the behest of a young peasant girl, the Hulk disposed of an evil tyrant and later battled the Mole Man to restore the sight of a young Russian. Aside from these acquaintances, the Hulk has also developed a few close friendships over the years…

Fred Sloan

Fred Sloan was a mild-mannered would-be writer who was drifting through life until he encountered the Hulk. After the Hulk saved Fred from a beating by some rednecks, Fred took an extended road trip with old Greenskin and eventually came to believe that the Hulk was harmless, unless provoked. Fred later wrote a book about his adventures entitled *Hulk Encounter: A Survivor's Story.*

Crackerjack Jackson

Crackerjack Jackson was a homeless vagrant who wandered the countryside. Drawn to Crackerjack's campsite by the sound of harmonica music, the Hulk was surprised when the old man welcomed him and offered to share his meager dinner. Crackerjack taught the Hulk how to eat with a fork and to spell his own name, but he was later killed by a pair of escaping convicts.

JIM WILSON

The youngest of all the Hulk's sidekicks, Jim Wilson was an orphan who never had a chance. Barely 14 years old when his parents died, Jim lived alone in a burned-out tenement and survived by stealing food. He gained the Hulk's trust by sharing his last candy bar. Though people say the Hulk is incapable of compassion, something about Jim touched a chord deep inside the greenskinned brute. They traveled together until Jim was reunited with a distant uncle. When Jim returned a few years later, the Hulk learned that his friend was dying. Even with all his power, the Hulk couldn't save Jim Wilson.

TURNING TO CRIME
Though he hated to do it, young Jim Wilson was on the verge of starvation and had to resort to petty theft just to survive.

BETTY ROSS

ELIZABETH "BETTY" ROSS was always daddy's girl. The only daughter of General Thaddeus "Thunderbolt" Ross and his wife Karen Lee, Betty was born on a military base in Southern California. She was a typical Air Force brat who moved to a different town every time her father was transferred. The family never stayed in one place long enough to put down any roots, so Betty didn't have many friends her own age. Her playmates were the airmen who worked under her father and were often assigned to watch her. Karen Lee died while Betty was a still teenager. Unable to cope with his own grief, General Ross claimed that a military base was no place for a young girl and sent Betty to boarding school. The spitting image of her mother, Betty rejoined her father after she graduated, moving into his quarters on the missile base. It was there she eventually met Bruce Banner.

LOVE AT FIRST SIGHT

Shortly after Dr. Banner arrived on General Ross's missile base, Betty introduced herself and officially welcomed him to his new home. The shy and sensitive scientist was different from the military men that usually surrounded Betty and a strong attraction immediately grew between them. When Betty learned that her father considered Banner to be a physical and emotional weakling, she rushed to his defense. She remained devoted to Banner even after he became the Hulk.

A MIND OF HER OWN
Betty Ross may have dressed the part of the perfect military daughter and deferred to her father in public, but she was a very different person behind closed doors. Strong-willed, confident and stubborn, Betty knew exactly what she wanted. She loved her father, but ignored his bluster and didn't allow him to dominate her life. The General's dislike of Bruce Banner may have only made him more appealing to her.

ON THE REBOUND
Though marred by the shadow of the Hulk, Betty's love grew for Bruce Banner. When he was reported dead, she was devastated. She turned to Major Glenn Talbot for support and they were soon married. She tried to make her marriage work, but Betty was still in love with Banner and eventually divorced Talbot.

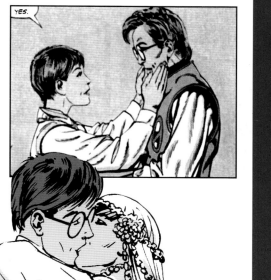

ON BENDED KNEE
When a process separated the Hulk and Banner into two different beings, Bruce thought he was cured and asked Betty to marry him. Fearing their happiness wouldn't last long, Betty trusted her heart and said yes.

THE FATHER OF THE BRIDE
The victim of a recent nervous breakdown, General Ross became furious when he learned of his daughter's plans. He tried to browbeat Betty into changing her mind. When that failed, he showed up at the ceremony with gun in hand, fully prepared to commit murder to prevent his only child from making such a horrible mistake. After wounding Rick Jones, Banner's best man, Ross was brought to his senses when Betty stood up to him.

Unhappily Ever After
Betty's secret misgivings about her marriage proved all too real, and, to survive, Bruce had to be reunited with the Hulk. She stood by her husband, but was horrified to learn that he sometimes triggered his transformations himself in order to battle certain menaces. The strain of being married to a raging monster often overwhelmed Betty. Yet though she would leave him for long periods of time, she always returned. She just couldn't help herself. Betty Ross loved Bruce Banner until the day she died.

YOU MAY HAVE **BRUTE STRENGTH**-- BUT I HAVE THE UNBRIDLED POWER OF THE **HARPY'S HELLBOLTS**--

Thin Line Between Love and Hate
While married to Glenn Talbot and desiring revenge on the Hulk (whom she blamed for Bruce's supposed death), Betty was captured by MODOK. He exposed her to gamma rays and turned her into the Harpy. Armed with razor-sharp claws, superhuman strength, and the ability to generate concussive blasts, she set out to destroy the Hulk. She almost succeeded because old Greenskin couldn't bring himself to harm the woman he still loved.

UNDEFEATED
The Harpy beat the Hulk by blasting him unconscious. Changing back into Bruce, he devised a way to expel her gamma radiation. She regained human form and never became the Harpy again.

THE OTHER WOMEN

> SO YOU'RE BRUCE BANNER...THE GENIUS THAT EVERYONE IN THE SCHOOL IS *BUZZING* ABOUT.

> WORD IS THAT YOU'RE HEADING FOR *GREAT* THINGS, BRUCE.

> OH, ME? I'M SUSAN JACOBSON.

Susan Jacobson

Susan first approached Banner at a college party. She had heard all about the boy genius and was curious to meet him. They began to date, but Banner scared her off because he would sometimes explode in a fit of temper and seem like someone else. Susan graduated college and became a covert operative for the C.I.A. When she was unfairly imprisoned for leaking government secrets, the Hulk broke her out of jail and guaranteed her safety.

BETTY ROSS MAY have been the only woman that Bruce Banner ever truly loved, but she wasn't the only woman in his life. Bruce was shy and awkward as a teenager. His first attempts at dating were more humiliating than satisfying and no girl ever accepted a second date. Tired of being a social outcast, Bruce made a real effort to change. At college, he treated dating like a scientific experiment and prepared by reading books and studying romantic movies. Some women found his bumbling attempts sweet and he actually started getting second and third dates. Bruce gradually grew more comfortable around women and even had a few serious relationships. After graduation, he became totally focused on his work and stopped dating until he met Betty Ross. These, however, are a few of the women who have mattered to the Hulk…

> HOWDY, HANDSOME.

> SOMETHING I CAN *DO* YOU FOR?

> WELL, I--AH-- SAW THE *SIGN* HANGING OUT IN FRONT AND...

> SAY NO MORE, SEXY. JUST FOLLOW *ME!*

> NOW THAT'S THE *NICEST* OFFER I'VE HEARD ALL DAY!

April Sommers

April Sommers was an unsuccessful model who watched over an old apartment building for a discount on her rent. She rented a room to Bruce Banner and even helped him find a job. April had a friendly personality. She thought mild-mannered Bruce was handsome and sexy. He invited her out for a steak dinner, but April panicked when she learned he was secretly the Hulk and ordered him to move out of her building.

BEREET

Originally from a distant planet called Krylor, Bereet was a techno-artist who learned about the Hulk and used him as a fictional character in a number of techno-adventure films without his knowledge. She considered the Hulk a celebrity and journeyed to Earth to document his real life. Bereet was immediately attracted to Bruce Banner, but he just ignored her. She helped the Hulk on a few occasions and filmed everything. Bereet eventually decided to stay on Earth and moved to Los Angeles where she directs action movies.

Sturky, a hovering device that could convert one form of matter into another, always accompanied Bereet.

Bereet traveled with a bag of props that could instantly expand into giant robots.

THE STAR EYE Bereet invented a machine called the Star Eye. It was an entertainment module that could film real events and add fictional elements to them. The result was a new techno-adventure movie. Bereet created a series of films that starred the Hulk.

> ...AND DOES HE ALWAYS GO FOR LONG WALKS ABOUT THE COUNTRYSIDE--

> --DRESSED ONLY IN A VERY BECOMING PAIR OF PURPLE SHORTS?

Kidnapped by the Abomination, Kate was briefly transformed into a female version of MODOK until the Hulk cured her.

Dr. Kate Waynesboro

At a time when the Hulk had Bruce Banner's intelligence, Dr. Kate Waynesboro became his research assistant and helped him study the effects of gamma radiation on the Earth. Banner did not know that she was a S.H.I.E.L.D. agent who had been assigned to keep an eye on the scientist. Kate grew to care for Banner and was horrified as the Hulk became more uncontrollable. When S.H.I.E.L.D. decided to terminate the Hulk, Kate refused to help and resigned.

> OH MY LORD!

> THAT'S WHAT I LIKE TO HEAR. RESPECT.

> HOLD IT. THAT WAS MY BEEPER. BE BACK IN A FEW MINUTES. YOU STAY *PUT.*

> UH...

> UH...

> OKAY.

BLIND DATE
Marlo's best friend was dating Las Vegas casino owner Michael Berengetti and offered to set her up on a blind date with the most eligible bachelor in town, the mysterious Joe Fixit.

Marlo Chandler

A former Las Vegas showgirl, Marlo Chandler began to date the Hulk while he was Joe Fixit. She met Bruce Banner, who claimed to be Joe's half-brother, and who warned her against falling in love with Joe. Marlo learned the truth about the Hulk and broke up with him. She later became friends with Betty Banner, then dated and married Rick Jones. They starred together in a television talk show called *Keeping Up With the Joneses* and Marlo used her share of the profits to buy a comic-book store.

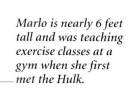

Marlo is nearly 6 feet tall and was teaching exercise classes at a gym when she first met the Hulk.

GENERAL ROSS

T HADDEUS E. ROSS was born to a family with a proud military tradition. His grandfather served under General Sherman in the American Civil War and his father became a highly decorated general during World War I. The first in his class at West Point, he married Karen Lee, the daughter of his commanding officer. Ross rose through the ranks and was stationed in the Pacific during World War II, where he established himself as a great military leader. After the war, he was briefly assigned to Los Alamos, New Mexico, where he met Dr. Brian Banner, Bruce's father. General Ross was assigned a desk job after the death of his wife and sent to command the missile base and nuclear research center known as Desert Base, New Mexico.

LIKE A THUNDERBOLT
Ross gained the nickname "Thunderbolt" because of the way he led his troops during World War II. It also suited his explosive personality. He had a hair-trigger temper and expected his orders to be carried out instantly. Ross believed in the military way of life and had little tolerance for civilians.

Personality Clash

Ross was outraged when Dr. Bruce Banner was sent by the government to oversee and test his new gamma or G-Bomb. The general resented the fact that a civilian was in charge of such an important military project and he had nothing but contempt for the scrawny scientist. To make matters worse, his daughter Betty seemed to be attracted to Banner.

AT WAR WITH THE HULK

When the Hulk first appeared, General Ross believed that the former Soviet Union had sent the monster to sabotage his missile base and even suspected Dr. Banner of being a foreign spy. Convinced that the Hulk was a threat to national security, Ross dedicated himself to capturing or killing the creature. His inability to complete this mission led to a series of nervous breakdowns that jeopardized his career and almost cost him his life. Ross was enraged when Betty finally married Bruce Banner. However, he was utterly devastated when she died a few years later from gamma-radiation poisoning.

MY SON-IN-LAW, THE MONSTER
General Ross came to sympathize with Banner's plight and no longer blames him for Betty's death.

COLONEL GLENN TALBOT

LIKE HIS MENTOR Thunderbolt Ross, Glenn Talbot was from a proud military family. His ancestors supported the Confederacy during the American Civil War and his father was a career officer who served in Europe during World War II. Talbot attended West Point, graduating near the top of his class. He decided to continue his education and study for a degree in military law. Talbot requested an assignment to the Criminal Investigation Division and solved a number of high-profile cases. Promoted to the rank of Major, Talbot was transferred to Desert Base, New Mexico, at the request of General Ross. Ross had begun to suspect that Dr. Banner, his chief scientist, was a traitor because he kept disappearing for long periods without explanation. The general also wanted Talbot to help him capture or destroy the Hulk, and thought the young officer might get his daughter's mind off Banner.

THE MAN BEHIND THE CURTAIN
Talbot became convinced that Banner was a spy when he vanished and later resurfaced behind the Iron Curtain. Talbot journeyed to Mongolia to rescue Banner, but only so that the scientist could stand trial for treason.

BITTER RIVALS

After it became known that Banner was the Hulk, Major Talbot found himself in a rather awkward position. He had fallen in love with the general's daughter, but knew that Betty only had eyes for Banner. When the scientist was believed dead at one point, Talbot married the grief-stricken Betty on the rebound. While on a secret mission to the former Soviet Union, Talbot was captured by the Gremlin and imprisoned until the Hulk managed to free him. Talbot returned to the U.S., but his relationship with Betty deteriorated and she asked him for a divorce.

SECOND CHOICE
Betty tried to be the perfect military wife, but Talbot was always haunted by the knowledge that he was her second choice. No matter what Betty said or did, Talbot believed that she was still in love with Bruce Banner.

Fallen Warrior

After a nervous breakdown rendered General Ross unfit for duty, Talbot was promoted to Colonel and given command of the missile base. Determined to get revenge for the breakdown of his marriage, he became obsessed with killing the Hulk. Talbot stole an experimental weapon called the War Wagon and was accidentally killed when he launched an unprovoked attack on the Hulk.

HULK HUNTERS

> GYRICH, IF THIS IS SOME SORT OF SICK JOKE, I'LL SEE YOU ROAST IN HELL FOR THIS.

> I THINK THAT'S PRETTY WELL ATTENDED TO ALREADY.

FEARING THE HULK might become an international menace, the Pentagon appointed General Ross as the head of *Operation: Hulk* and ordered him to find, capture, or kill the creature. Ross captured Banner on several occasions, but no conventional prison could hold the Hulk. Realizing he needed a special facility in order to contain the creature, Ross petitioned the government for the necessary funds. The Pentagon responded by building a military base in the New Mexico desert that came to be known as the Hulkbuster Base. The military operation was now called *Operation: Greenskin* and its new mandate was to capture the Hulk and find a way to cure him and anyone else who had been exposed to gamma radiation.

GAMMA BASE

After the first Hulkbuster Base was destroyed during the course of a battle between the Hulk and a creature called the Devastator, the Pentagon replaced it with a new and improved facility called Gamma Base. Under *Project: Greenskin*, the government studied the effects of gamma radiation on the human body. Aside from General Ross and Colonel Talbot, a number of other people were assigned the daunting task of capturing the Hulk…

Henry Peter Gyrich
Gyrich was a special agent appointed by the National Security Council to investigate the Avengers and to upgrade the team's security procedures. He was later transferred to *Project: Wideawake*, a covert government commission that had been established to study and deal with the problems posed by the growing number of mutants in America.

ENLISTING THE HULK
Answering to the U.S. President, Gyrich was sent to decide if the Hulk posed a threat to national security. Gyrich also had the option of trying to enlist the Hulk's aid against mutant criminals.

Quiet and unassuming, Gyrich is dedicated to protecting the public from super-menaces.

> RIFLES UP HE'S MINE.

> CAREFUL, GENERAL.

St. Lawrence first met General Ross while she was a student at West Point, but he ignored her because he didn't approve of women cadets.

Colonel Cary St. Lawrence
Cary St. Lawrence was a military officer determined to prove that she was as tough and as efficient as any man. She graduated third in her class at West Point and was assigned directly to the Pentagon. When other efforts to capture the Hulk failed, Colonel St. Lawrence volunteered to go after the creature. She tracked him across the country and took him into custody at Flagstaff, Arizona. She came to respect the Hulk and treated him with kindness and affection.

SACRIFICE PLAY
Armbruster died a hero, sacrificing his own life to save the President of the United States

Colonel John D. Armbruster

When the Gremlin's Super-Soldiers took General Ross prisoner, Colonel Armbruster led the rescue mission. Armbruster replaced Ross as commander of *Project: Greenskin* and was in charge when the Abomination and the Rhino attacked Gamma Base. He captured Banner with a tranquilizer gun and later uncovered a plot to assassinate the President.

Colonel Nick Fury

A highly decorated hero who had been stationed in England during World War II, Nick Fury served in the C.I.A. for several years. He was later chosen to lead an international espionage organization called S.H.I.E.L.D. Fury considered the Hulk a threat to international security and always kept tabs on the monster.

Clay Quartermain

Quartermain was a S.H.I.E.L.D. agent who volunteered to serve as liaison with *Project: Greenskin*. He became friends with Doc Samson and Bruce Banner but was reassigned after the Leader detonated the gamma bomb that incinerated Middletown.

PERSONAL VENDETTA
Matt Talbot believed his Uncle Glenn was a hero who died trying to protect the U.S. from the Hulk. Matt hated Betty Ross for breaking Glenn's heart. He also held her responsible for his uncle's death.

Major Matt Talbot

Matt Talbot was a man with a grudge. He was determined to vindicate his uncle's name and punish the Hulk for the death of Colonel Glenn Talbot. Possessing a talent for zeroing in on an opponent's weakness, Matt was willing to go to any lengths to capture his uncle's former rival. He drew the Hulk out of hiding by shooting Betty in the leg with a stun pistol. His superiors were so shocked by his callous disregard for the law that they court-martialed him.

HULK IN THE 1960s

CHANGE HAS ALWAYS typified the Hulk. Created by Stan Lee and his long time collaborator Jack Kirby, the character was gray in his first issue and only came out at night. In his second issue, the Hulk became green, because Stan had noticed that the printer couldn't seem to supply a consistent shade of gray and the Hulk's skin color varied from page to page.

By his third issue, the Hulk could appear during the day, but was permanently stuck in his monster form and controlled by Rick Jones. Bruce Banner returned in the fourth issue, but now needed a machine to transform into the Hulk. All these changes may have confused readers because Stan soon decided to cancel the Hulk's comic. Artist Steve Ditko was drafted in to draw the jolly green giant's sixth and seemingly final issue.

However Stan Lee still had faith in the Hulk and included him in the lineup of Earth's mightiest heroes when The Avengers debuted a few months later. Realizing that the Hulk was not a team player, Stan recast the misunderstood monster as a recurring menace who guest-starred in *The Avengers*, *The Fantastic Four*, and *The Amazing Spider-Man*. The Hulk was soon awarded another series. Appearing in ten-page stories in *Tales To Astonish*, the Hulk's adventures were illustrated by Steve Ditko, Jack Kirby, Bob Powell, John Romita, Bill Everett, John Buscema, and Gil Kane.

Marie Severin finally took over the art chores with *Tales To Astonish #92* and continued until the next big change in the Hulk's life. Ending its run with its 101st outing, *Tales To Astonish* became *The Incredible Hulk* with the very next issue. While Marie remained the artist in residence, Gary Friedrich became the Hulk's new writer with an occasional assist from Archie Goodwin and Roy Thomas. Stan eventually returned to script his creation, though he later relinquished the writing reins to Roy Thomas in the waning months of 1969.

The Hulk was finally given his first taste of true stability when Herb Trimpe joined the series. Herb began his tenure by embellishing Marie Severin's highly illustrative pencils. He became the Hulk's main artist and remained on the title for over eight years.

The Avengers #1 *(Sept. 1963): After being hounded for most of the issue, the Hulk joins the team. (Cover by Jack Kirby)*

The Fantastic Four #12 *(March 1963): The Hulk meets and battles Marvel's first family.(Cover by Jack Kirby)*

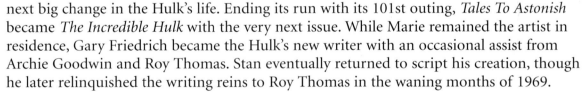

1962

The Incredible Hulk #1 *(May 1962): Old greenskin's first appearance. (Cover by Jack Kirby)*

1963

The Incredible Hulk #6 *(March 1963): The last issue of the Hulk's first volume. (Cover by Steve Ditko)*

1964

Tales To Astonish #60 *(Oct. 1964): The Hulk is given a second chance to star in his own series. (Cover by Jack Kirby)*

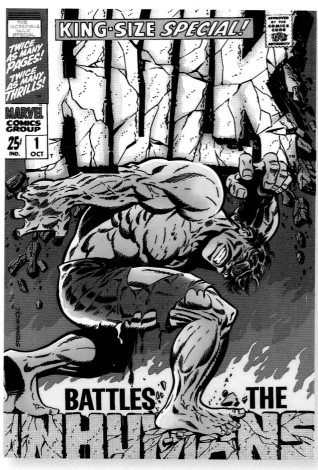

The Incredible Hulk Annual #1 *(1968):*
The Hulk meets the Inhumans in his very
first annual. (Cover by Marie Severin)

The Amazing Spider-Man Annual #3
(1966): Although they had met once
before, the Hulk battles Spider-Man.
(Cover by John Romita)

1966

Tales To Astonish
#77 (March 1966):
The Hulk's secret
identity is revealed
to the world. (Cover
by Jack Kirby)

1968

The Incredible
Hulk #102 *(April*
1968): The second
volume of the Hulk
continues for nearly
32 years. (Cover by
Marie Severin)

1969

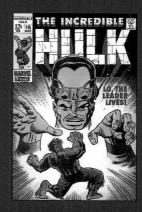

The Incredible
Hulk #108 *(March*
1969): The Leader
returns. (Cover by
Herb Trimpe)

THE RINGMASTER

THIS MASTER SHOWMAN loves entertaining audiences almost as much as robbing them. Maynard Tiboldt was born in Vienna, Austria to a family that ran a traveling circus. Replacing his father as ringmaster, Maynard moved the business to the US. However his small circus could not compete with much larger troupes, so he turned to crime. He built a device that enabled him to hypnotize the spectators; his performers then removed their valuables. The mesmerised crowd was then given a post-hypnotic suggestion to remove all memory of the robbery.

STARTING OVER
After his parents were murdered, Maynard Tiboldt fled Europe with his small circus. His show floundered in America until he realized that he could use hypnosis to gain the riches he desired.

The Ringmaster's top hat is equipped with a revolving disc that can hypnotize crowds or create illusions.

THE MONSTER OF THE AGE

By changing the name of his circus and sticking to small towns, the Ringmaster stayed ahead of the law until Rick Jones attended a performance. The Ringmaster soon had both Rick and the Hulk under his spell. Billing him as "The Monster of the Age", Maynard turned the Hulk into a sideshow attraction until he snapped out of his trance and brought the curtain down on the Circus Of Crime.

UNCONTROLLABLE RAGE
Not even the Ringmaster can hypnotize the Hulk when he's full of rage.

Helping the Hulk

During his criminal career, the Ringmaster has battled heroes like Spider-Man, the She-Hulk and Thor. Maynard was eventually sentenced to a long prison term. To win an early release, he volunteered to help Doc Samson cure the Hulk by using his hypnotic powers to merge all the different personalities of Bruce Banner and the Hulk into a single and stable individual.

THE CIRCUS OF CRIME
The Ringmaster's regular troupe are: Eliot "Crafty" Franklin (the clown), Bruce "Bruto" Olafsen (the circus strongman), Ernesto and Luigi Gambonno (acrobats and aerialists), Jack Pulver (the Human Cannonball) and Zelda DuBois, the beautiful snake charmer known as Princess Python.

DISC MAN
The Ringmaster recently underwent an operation that implanted hypnotic disks in his eyes. He can now mesmerize an individual on his own, but still needs his hat for multiple victims.

TYRANNUS™

H E WAS BORN TO RULE. His real name is Romulus Augustus and he is the last true Roman Emperor. Deposed in 476 AD when a child, Tyrannus believed destiny had cheated him. Determined to win back his empire, he raised a mighty army and tried to conquer England. He was defeated and captured by the legendary King Arthur and his Knights of the Round Table. Merlin the Magician banished Tyrannus to Subterranea, a vast network of caverns miles beneath the Earth's surface. Tyrannus soon discovered a race of subhuman creatures living underground. They became his willing slaves and gave him a precious gift—*the secret of immortality*!

THOUGH I WAS BANISHED TO THE CENTER OF EARTH CENTURIES AGO BY THE ACCURSED MERLIN THE MAGICIAN, THIS MAGIC ELIXER HAS KEPT ME ALIVE AND YOUNG ALL THESE YEARS-- WHILE I PLANNED MY REVENGE UPON MANKIND!

TYRANNUS DRINKS THE POTION! GREAT IS TYRANNUS! BOW DOWN TO THE ALL-POWERFUL TYRANNUS!

The Fountain of Youth
Shortly after he arrived, the Subterraneans took Tyrannus to an underground spring. The waters somehow possessed the magical ability to preserve his youth, strength, and vitality. He was now virtually immortal and had plenty of time to consolidate his underground kingdom and plan revenge on the surface world.

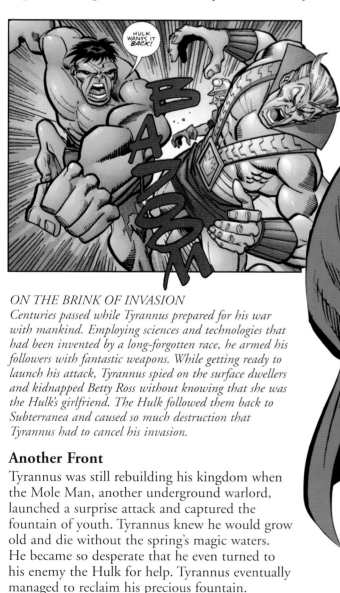

HULK WANTS IT BACK!

ON THE BRINK OF INVASION
Centuries passed while Tyrannus prepared for his war with mankind. Employing sciences and technologies that had been invented by a long-forgotten race, he armed his followers with fantastic weapons. While getting ready to launch his attack, Tyrannus spied on the surface dwellers and kidnapped Betty Ross without knowing that she was the Hulk's girlfriend. The Hulk followed them back to Subterranea and caused so much destruction that Tyrannus had to cancel his invasion.

Another Front
Tyrannus was still rebuilding his kingdom when the Mole Man, another underground warlord, launched a surprise attack and captured the fountain of youth. Tyrannus knew he would grow old and die without the spring's magic waters. He became so desperate that he even turned to his enemy the Hulk for help. Tyrannus eventually managed to reclaim his precious fountain.

Tyrannus has extensive knowledge of alchemy and engineering and is a brilliant strategist.

MOLE MAN™

A Lust for Revenge
No one knows the Mole's Man real name. According to legend he was a nearsighted and lonely man whose homely appearance caused him to be insulted or ignored ever since childhood. Disgusted with the way people treated him, he decided to exile himself from humanity. His travels eventually led to the underground world of Subterranea where, like Tyrannus, he soon established a little kingdom and began to feed his lust for vengeance.

IT HAS BEEN QUITE SOME TIME SINCE LAST YOU WERE A "GUEST" OF-- THE MOLE MAN!*

MOLE... MAN?

AH--YOU ARE SURPRISED TO SEE ME ALIVE, I TAKE IT? I SUPPOSE THAT IS TO BE EXPECTED!

TRAPPED BETWEEN TYRANTS
Though he has often been used as a pawn in the continuing underground war between the Mole Man and Tyrannus, the Hulk just wants to be left alone and really doesn't care who rules Subterranea.

THE AVENGERS ™

The Avengers team logo: a sign of hope and trust.

THEY ARE THE EARTH'S mightiest heroes, gathering together whenever the planet is threatened by a super-menace too powerful for any single hero. Though its roster is constantly changing, the founding members of the team consisted of the mighty Thor, the invincible Iron Man, the astonishing Ant-Man, the wondrous Wasp, and the incredible Hulk. How did such a motley group come to assemble? The answer lies on distant Asgard, the legendary home of the Norse Gods. Loki, the Norse God of evil, had been exiled to the dreaded Isle of Silence for plotting against his half-brother, Thor. Desperate for revenge, Loki needed to find a way to draw the thunder god back to Asgard. Spotting the Hulk, the Asgardian mischief-maker used a magic spell to trick him into destroying a train trestle.

The invincible Iron Man was secretly Tony Stark, a multi-millionaire industrialist who designed and built an armored suit equipped with highly sophisticated weaponry.

American biochemist Dr. Henry Pym discovered a serum that could drastically alter his size. He began his super hero career as the Ant-Man but changed his name to Giant-Man.

Loki made the Hulk think that dynamite had been placed on the train tracks. When the Hulk reached for it, he crashed into the trestle.

The Teen Brigade

Fearing that the Hulk was on another rampage, Rick Jones summoned his newly formed Teen Brigade and attempted to contact the Fantastic Four by short-wave radio. Loki, however, redirected Rick's message to Thor. Unfortunately for the god of evil, Iron Man, Ant-Man, and the Wasp also heard the teen's plea for help and quickly responded. Soon after the heroes met with the Teen Brigade, Thor began to suspect that Loki was trying to frame the Hulk.

THE CULPRIT REVEALED
While the other heroes went after the Hulk, Thor journeyed to the Isle of Silence where he battled Loki and eventually learned the truth. After the thunder god revealed the Hulk's innocence, the five heroes decided to put aside their differences and work together as… the Avengers!

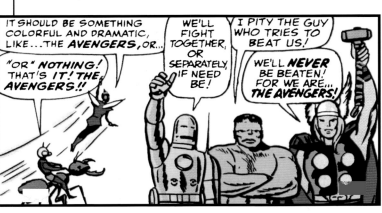

The Norse god of thunder, Thor is the lord of the storm and wields an enchanted hammer called Mjolnir.

Though she eventually married Henry Pym, Janet Van Dyne became the Ant-Man's partner when he gave her the ability to grow wasp-like wings whenever she shrunk to insect-size.

Always the Outsider

Though he was sick of being hunted and hounded and preferred to join the Avengers rather than fight them, the Hulk never truly fitted in with the rest of the team. Thor was repulsed by the way he came to their regular meetings dressed only in a pair of trunks and Iron Man took offense at the Hulk's surly and sullen personality. Before too long, the Hulk was constantly arguing with the other heroes, and they began to regret including him on the team.

THE SPACE PHANTOM
An alien invader known as the Space Phantom realized he could use this discord to destroy the team. He used his shape-changing ability to impersonate the Hulk. The boastful Space Phantom revealed his plans to Rick Jones.

THE ENEMY WITHIN
The Space Phantom presumed that a mere teenager like Rick would pose no threat to his schemes. However, when the Phantom masqueraded as the Hulk and started a fight with the other Avengers, Rick told all.

THE ORDER CHANGETH
Once they learned the truth, the Avengers eventually defeated the Space Phantom, but the story didn't end happily! Hurt and angry that his teammates had been so quick to band against him, the Hulk refused to accept their apologies and quit the Avengers.

BETRAYED!

Fearing what the Hulk might do on his own, the remaining Avengers mounted a nationwide search for him and even tried to enlist the aid of Spider-Man, the Fantastic Four, and the X-Men. It was Rick Jones who finally found him. Realizing the Hulk was completely out of control, Rick contacted the Avengers and told them where the Hulk was hiding. The Hulk managed to evade his former teammates, learned of Rick's betrayal, and decided he could no longer trust the teenager. Many years would pass before they became friends again.

If you don't know who the Hulk is by now, you're definitely reading the wrong book!

CAPTAIN AMERICA
Soon after the Hulk quit the team, the Avengers found a living legend from World War II who had been frozen in a block of ice: Captain America. A super-athlete, Cap is a master of all forms of hand to hand combat and a brilliant strategist. His only weapon is a shield made of a unique metal alloy that makes it practically indestructible. The Avengers invited Cap to replace the Hulk and he eventually became team leader.

FRIENDLY FIRE

Armed with his enchanted Uru hammer, Thor is one of the few super heroes who can equal the raw power of the Hulk.

THE HULK'S BAD TEMPER and caustic wit are always getting him into trouble. He not only has an army of bad guys lining up to destroy him, he also picks fights with people who should be his friends. He began this bad habit when he met the Fantastic Four. Someone was sabotaging General Ross's base and the Hulk was the main suspect. Ross asked the super hero team for help. Instead of working with the F.F., the Hulk started a fight with them. He then joined the Avengers, claiming he was tired of fighting other super heroes. However his decision to quit the team led to a battle with the mighty Thor.

Thor, Norse god of thunder, wondered who was stronger and who would win in a fight—the Hulk or him.

COMING TO BLOWS
Thor learned the answers to these questions one day when the Hulk was fighting the Avengers and the two of them got separated from the others. Thor wished to face the Hulk on equal terms and used an ancient spell that allowed him to discard his magic hammer.

THE GOD AND THE MONSTER

To see who was the more powerful, Thor and the Hulk quickly engaged in hand-to-hand battle. The thunder god was taken aback by the Hulk's unrelenting fury. He was also shocked to learn that the Hulk could shrug off his greatest blows and seemed to grow stronger with each passing moment. It soon became obvious that the Hulk possessed far greater strength and endurance. Yet Thor, a warrior born of Asgard and trained in all manner of combat, was more skilled and experienced as a fighter and the battle eventually ended in a stalemate.

Having the advantage of surprise, the Hulk gets in the first blow, a thundering left which could fell a bull elephant! But the Thing is merely toppled off balance for a second...

ARGHHH! It's like hitting a STONE WALL!

POW!

YEP, *UUGGNN*—IT'S *TOO LATE*, AL'RIGHT!

STUPID PILE OF ORANGE ROCKS—HULK WILL *SMASH!*

WHOOM!

When Monsters Clash

With Reed Richards (Mr. Fantastic), Johnny Storm (the Human Torch) and Susan Richards (the Invisible Woman), Benjamin J. Grimm formed the Fantastic Four. Ben first became the monstrous mass of muscle known as the Thing when he and his friends were accidentally exposed to cosmic rays. The ever-loving, blue-eyed idol of millions has fought the Hulk on numerous occasions and has learned that he cannot match the greenskinned giant's power or ferocity. But Ben is a street fighter from the slums of New York and he's far too stubborn to ever admit defeat.

SIGNS OF BATTLE
The Hulk and the Thing have battled from the deserts of New Mexico to the streets of Manhattan and bashful Benjamin has the bruises to prove it.

Wild and Webby

Bitten by a radioactive spider, Peter Parker gained the proportionate strength, speed, and agility of the dying arachnid. However, he quickly realized that he couldn't match the power of the Hulk. The Amazing Spider-Man first ran into the Hulk by accident in an underground cave and barely managed to avoid getting clobbered.

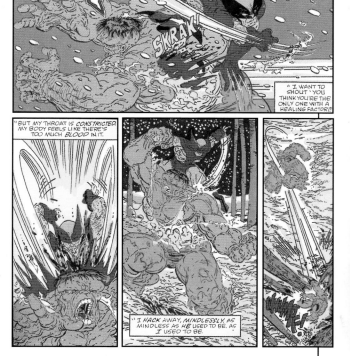

ARR-RARH

" BUT I'M NO *SLOUCH* MYSELF

SKRAK!

" I WANT TO SHOUT " YOU THINK YOU'RE THE ONLY ONE WITH A *HEALING FACTOR!!*

" BUT MY THROAT IS *CONSTRICTED,* MY BODY FEELS LIKE THERE'S TOO MUCH *BLOOD* IN IT.

" I HACK AWAY, *MINDLESSLY,* AS MINDLESS AS *HE* USED TO BE, AS *I* USED TO BE

THKOW

I DID IT! I STAGGERED THE *HULK!!*

SPEED OVER STRENGTH
Spider-Man uses his agility to keep out of reach until he can line up the perfect punch—even if it usually hurts him *more than the Hulk!*

CLAWS MAKE THE MUTANT
Possessing a pair a razor-sharp metal claws, an uncanny ability to heal from almost any injury, superhuman strength, and super-enhanced senses, Wolverine is as deadly as his name implies. It has taken him years to master his berserker rages, but he may still be the only one who can equal the Hulk's unbridled savagery.

THE **LEADER**™

The Leader has a photographic memory and can read over 4,000 words a minute.

L IKE BRUCE BANNER, Samuel Sterns was accidentally exposed to a huge dose of gamma radiation. But instead of gaining incredible physical strength, he acquired a superhuman mind. His hunger for knowledge became insatiable. Calling himself the Leader, he sent scientists to spy on U.S. government research facilities. The more secrets he learned, the less he trusted the government. Sterns decided that only he was smart enough to rule the world. His attempt to steal Dr. Bruce Banner's radiation secrets led to his first confrontation with the Hulk. Sterns suspected that the monster's great strength was the result of gamma rays and plotted to enslave him and exploit his physical power. He captured the Hulk and subjected him to a variety of tests. However, Sterns soon realized that no one can ever truly control the Hulk and has tried to destroy him ever since.

BRAWN OVER BRAINS

The Hulk has thwarted the Leader's plans for world conquest time and again. Sterns once seized control of General Ross's missile base and would have started a nuclear war if the Hulk hadn't intervened. On another occasion, Sterns tried to take over the U.S. government by making android duplicates of the President and Vice-President.

THE ACCIDENTAL GENIUS
Samuel Sterns was a high-school dropout. He was working as a manual laborer in a government-owned research facility when he was accidentally bombarded by gamma rays. Sterns somehow survived and appeared to be unharmed.

GETTING AHEAD
While recovering from his accident, Sterns began to read every book he could get his hands on. His intellect expanded at an astounding rate as he absorbed knowledge like a sponge. To accommodate his growing brain, his head increased to almost five times its former size. He became an expert in every field of science and technology, specializing in robotics, genetics, and nuclear research. He also found that he could project illusions into the minds of his enemies, though he had difficulty controlling anyone who had also been exposed to gamma rays.

Since the Leader's entire body is covered with gamma-induced bumps and boils, he wears special cushioned boots and a uniform that has been padded for maximum comfort.

AN ARMY OF ANDROIDS

The Leader designed robots called humanoids to replace his human lackeys. These powerful machines possessed super-strength and a resilient sponge-like outer shell that could absorb almost any attack. They were also equipped with various weapons and ranged from microscopic sizes to hundreds of feet tall.

The Leader sits in his lab, preparing to unleash his terrifying Humanoid on an unsuspecting world.

The Final Farewell

The war between the Leader and the Hulk continued for years. Sterns only survived thanks to a series of machines he had built that revived his gamma-irradiated body. Unfortunately, these same machines mutated him—until he lost all resemblance to humanity. Realizing he was about to transcend the physical world, Sterns sought out the Hulk for a final meeting. To the Hulk's surprise, he no longer wished to conquer the world. The Leader just wanted to spend his last moments in the company of the one man who truly understood him. Yet, though he appeared to die, it's always possible that the Leader may return.

The Leader's Utopia

Believing that it was only a matter of time before mankind wiped itself out, the Leader stopped trying to conquer the world and decided to establish his own kingdom. He built Freehold, a utopia-like city beneath an iceberg in Alberta, Canada. By offering some of the world's greatest scientists unlimited funds for research, he enticed them to join him. He also sought out people who were sick or dying or had lost hope with the outside world. He promised them that their descendants would one day emerge from Freehold and turn the rest of the Earth into a paradise. Unfortunately, Hydra, a terrorist organization dedicated to world domination, learned of Freehold's existence and attempted to conquer it. Even though the Hulk hated the idea of helping his old enemy, he arrived in time to drive the invaders away.

SAFE HAVEN surrounded by ice, the city of Freehold believed that it was totally secluded and safe from the outside world.

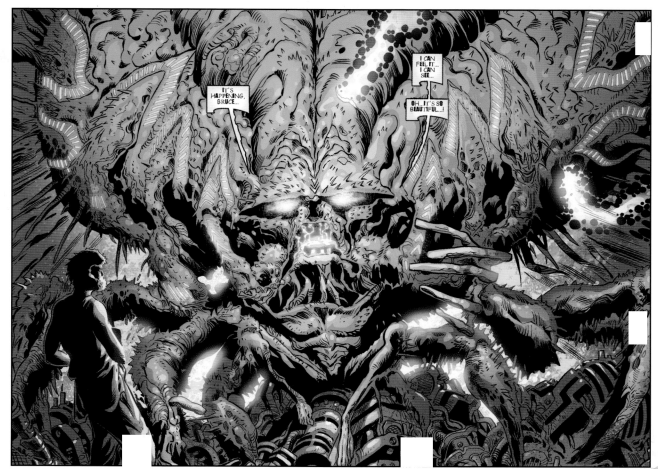

BOOMERANG™

FRED MYERS IS A MAN who enjoys the good life. He dresses in fine clothes, lives in a plush apartment, dines in the finest restaurants and dates a bevy of beautiful women. Fred was born in northern Australia where he learned the art of throwing a boomerang as a child. After moving to America, he fell in love with baseball and eventually became a professional player. He enjoyed a brilliant career as a pitcher in the minor leagues, moved into the majors, but was suspended for taking bribes. Fearing that he was finished as ballplayer, Fred decided to turn his skills toward crime. He designed an arsenal of throwing weapons and became a mercenary. Code-named Boomerang by a criminal organization called the Secret Empire, Fred was hired to steal an experimental missile from General Ross's base. He took Betty Ross hostage and offered to exchange her for the missile's plans.

A WALKING ARSENAL
Boomerang's costume is composed of light body armor and contains hidden weapons pockets. His metal disks can cut through solid steel. He also has boomerangs that are rigged with special gimmicks, like his "shatterangs" that explode with the force of 20 hand grenades, and tear-gas "gasarangs."

Battle Cry of the Boomerang!
The Hulk rushed to Betty's aid. Boomerang believed his weapons made him unbeatable, but Fred soon learned the error of his ways and was forced to flee for his life. Determined to get revenge, Boomerang polished his skills and improved his weaponry. Shattering the wall of a nearby dam, Fred attempted to drown the Hulk in a raging flood. While an over-confident Boomerang taunted him, the Hulk used the last vestiges of his strength to smash a nearby mountain and save himself.

RETURN ENGAGEMENT

Frustrated by his inability to beat a mindless beast like the Hulk, Fred returned to Australia. He designed a new costume and upgraded his weaponry. He later returned to the U.S. and became a fulltime assassin. During the course of his career, Boomerang often battled the amazing Spider-Man and even challenged Iron Man and the Defenders. A dying gang lord learned that Bruce Banner was developing a way to use gamma rays to cure cancer. He hired Fred to force the scientist to test the rays on him. Boomerang accepted the job and, like his namesake, was soon sent flying back to jail.

UNERRING ACCURACY
Any small object is a weapon in the hands of Boomerang and he never misses his target. He is ambidextrous and equally dangerous with either hand.

Boomerang's boot jets can propel him through the air or be used as weapons against pursing enemies.

Qnax, hailed as the greatest fighter in the universe, emerges from his watery lair to go Hulk hunting.

QNAX™

CHAMPION FIGHTER
Qnax is as strong as the Hulk and expert in all forms of armed and unarmed combat. He can also breathe underwater and swim at superhuman speed.

HE IS THE MOST POWERFUL CREATURE IN THE GALAXY! AND, ONLY BY DEFEATING HIM CAN YOU RETURN TO EARTH! EVERYTHING DEPENDS ON THE NEXT FEW SECONDS!

HOW ...HOW LONG HAVE I--?

YOU DON'T WANT TO KNOW.

BORN ON THE PLANET XANTARES, Qnax is the product of centuries of scientific breeding to produce the ultimate fighting machine. He spent most of his life training for combat or brawling in the public arenas. When chaos threatened his homeworld, the Grand Xantarean Council of Elders chose Qnax to secure a device that could return order to their crumbling civilization. They sent him to the planet of the Watchers to steal the Sphere of Ultimate Knowledge. The Hulk had also been sent to retrieve the Sphere. Qnax had never tasted defeat and expected a quick victory, but the Hulk grew stronger as the battle raged. Qnax moved the fight to a nearby lake where he thought he'd have an advantage and trapped the Hulk in a fissure beneath the water's surface. But the Hulk broke free and hurled Qnax into space.

THE CHAMPION REBORN

After the Galaxy Master's overthrow, Qnax resumed his exploration of the universe. He saw many wonders and finally gained humility. He also decided to try to complete his original mission and secure the Sphere of Ultimate Knowledge for his people. This time he tried working with the Hulk instead of against him. They journeyed back to the world of the Watchers and were eventually allowed to enter the Sphere. Qnax learned that the Council of Elders had played him for a fool. Instead of using the Sphere to save his fellow Xantareans, the Council wanted its power to dominate them.

Shanghaied in Space

Qnax returned to Xantares in disgrace. The Council of Elders condemned him for his failure to secure the Sphere and sentenced him to permanent exile. Working as a freelance gladiator, he journeyed across the universe until he came to the attention of an alien Empress who was attempting to destroy a monstrous creature called the Galaxy Master. Qnax was only able to help her achieve this feat with the aid of his former enemy the Hulk, a robot warrior named Torgo, and the reptilian Dark-Crawler.

After hating the Hulk for many years, Qnax grew to respect Bruce Banner and even saved his life on a few occasions (while they were attempting to secure the Sphere of Ultimate Knowledge).

THE ABOMINATION™

A HEAVY DOSE
Thanks to Banner's machine, Emil Blonsky received a massive dose of gamma radiation. Somehow, he survived and mutated into the monstrous Abomination.

HOW DO YOU FIGHT someone who is bigger, stronger, and usually smarter? That's the problem the Hulk faces every time he battles the Abomination. Though the webbed-eared, snake-eyed monster was originally shorter and weighed a little less than the Hulk, the Abomination has grown taller and more massive over the years. He now stands a full head taller than the Hulk and possesses slightly more superhuman strength, stamina, and durability than old greenskin. The Abomination can easily lift 100 tons and is practically impervious to pain, injury, and disease. Bruce Banner's own feelings of guilt make the Abomination even more difficult for the Hulk to defeat—for Banner blames himself for the accident that created the Abomination.

Body covered with lizard-like scales.

BRAWN WITH BRAINS
The Hulk was taken by surprise the first time he fought the Abomination. Not only could he stand up to the Hulk's attacks, the Abomination could launch his own onslaughts. Unlike the Hulk, Emil's mind was unaffected by his transformation. He retained his natural intelligence and superior knowledge of hand-to-hand combat.

Powerful leg muscles allow him to leap great distances, covering a few miles with each bound.

COMES THE MONSTER!

Born in Zagreb, Yugoslavia, Emil Blonsky liked to make up stories. Instead of becoming a writer, he sought power by becoming a spy. He rose quickly through the ranks and was assigned to infiltrate an air force base in the US. His handlers had learned that Bruce Banner was the Hulk, and Emil was sent to spy on the scientist and learn the secrets of gamma radiation. Unknown to Emil, Banner had decided to commit suicide in order to save the world from the Hulk. He built a machine that would bombard him with enough gamma radiation to kill his alter ego. That's when fate intervened! Banner was arrested moments before he could activate the machine. Not realizing the machine's true purpose, Emil decided to test it on himself. Instead of killing Emil, Banner's machine transformed him into the Abomination.

Beauty and the Beast

Emil Blonsky met and married beautiful actress Nadia Dornova a few years before he was sent to the United States. After he became the Abomination, Emil desperately wanted to be reunited with her, but decided it would be best if she believed he was dead. Though he has often questioned this decision, the Abomination has never revealed his true identity to Nadia.

I NEVER MISS!

WASTING AWAY
The Hulk once hurled the Abomination into some toxic waste containers. The deadly chemicals melted parts of his body, but his gamma-irradiated metabolism eventually healed him.

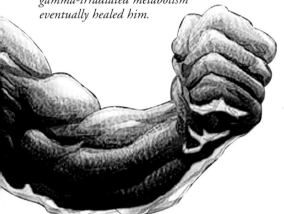

In contrast to the Hulk, the Abomination rarely changes back into Emil Blonsky.

The Abomination's skin can withstand blistering heat and freezing cold. He cannot be injured by small-arms fire and can even shrug off an exploding bazooka shell.

Timing is Everything!
The Abomination's superior physical strength gives him a distinct advantage over the Hulk at the start of every fight. However, the Hulk's strength increases as he gets angrier, but the Abomination's remains the same. The longer a battle lasts, the stronger the Hulk grows and the more the odds turn in his favor.

NNOOO!

MODOK™

Designed for Killing
MODOK's name stands for "Mobile Organism Designed Only for Killing," yet he was once an ordinary man: George Tarleton, a technician working for a secret organization known as AIM or Advanced Idea Mechanics. An experiment in controlled mutation required a guinea pig and George was bio-engineered into a large-headed creature with a superhuman mind and psionic powers. MODOK used his powers to take over AIM and soon began making plans for world conquest.

YOU SHALL NEVER BE ALONE AGAIN, ABOMINATION! WHEREVER YOU GO YOU SHALL CARRY WITH YOU THE TERROR INSTILLED BY MODOK!

BUT, LIKE THE HULK, I, TOO, HAVE NO MORE TIME FOR YOU!

Fearing that the Hulk might interfere with his plans for conquest, MODOK once captured and brainwashed Blonsky, hoping to use him as a pawn against the greenskinned goliath. MODOK quickly discovered that no one can control the Abomination or stop the Hulk.

THE RHINO™

Rhino versus Hulk: the incredible feels the full force of the unstoppable.

THE HULK AT BAY
The Rhino once formed a brief partnership with the Abomination. They attacked General Ross's missile base and took everyone captive. Their plan was to lure the Hulk into a trap and use the base's resources to destroy him. The Hulk was caught between two of his strongest foes, but kept fighting.

THE RHINO POSSESSES superhuman strength and is incredibly fast for someone his size and weight. He's almost impervious to pain and can run for hours at a time. He can achieve a top speed of nearly a 100 mph, and is virtually unstoppable once he reaches ramming mode. He smashes through concrete buildings and leaves a trail of twisted cars and shattered trucks in his wake. Though he currently goes by the name of Alex O'Hirn, he was once a Russian immigrant who worked as hired muscle for debt collecting or robberies. Foreign spies recruited him and offered to transform him into an invincible, superhuman agent. Since he needed the money to bring his relatives out of Eastern Europe, he agreed to become the Rhino.

The Rhino's horns are razor-sharp and can easily rip through solid steel.

Constructed of thick layers of polymer, his bodysuit is like the hide of a real rhinoceros, tough, coarse, and highly resistant to damage.

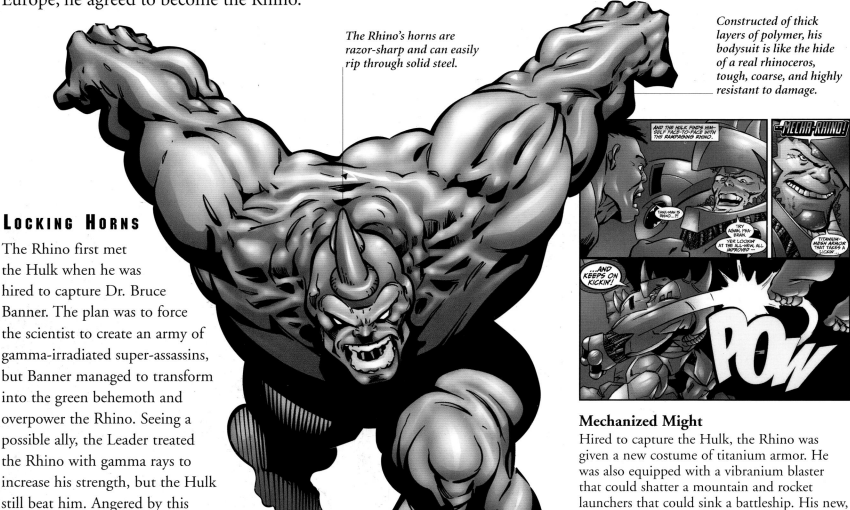

LOCKING HORNS

The Rhino first met the Hulk when he was hired to capture Dr. Bruce Banner. The plan was to force the scientist to create an army of gamma-irradiated super-assassins, but Banner managed to transform into the green behemoth and overpower the Rhino. Seeing a possible ally, the Leader treated the Rhino with gamma rays to increase his strength, but the Hulk still beat him. Angered by this failure, the Leader mentally seized control of the Rhino's body, attacked the Hulk and tried to strand them both in outer space.

Mechanized Might
Hired to capture the Hulk, the Rhino was given a new costume of titanium armor. He was also equipped with a vibranium blaster that could shatter a mountain and rocket launchers that could sink a battleship. His new, titanium-tipped horn was sharp enough to cut diamonds. His strength was nearly doubled and his speed increased to over 500 mph. Full of confidence, the all-new Rhino cornered the Hulk in a deserted amusement park and was promptly beaten into submission. The Rhino has never yet defeated the Hulk.

THE SANDMAN™

WILLIAM BAKER was raised in a New York City slum and learned to steal almost as soon as he could walk. Expelled from high school for fixing football games, Baker found steady work as a leg breaker for a local mobster. He was feared throughout the New York underworld and arrested several times. After a daring jailbreak, Baker hid in a deserted military base until the authorities gave up looking for him. He didn't realize that the site had been abandoned so that the military could test a new nuclear weapon. Lying on a nearby beach, Baker was caught in the bomb's blast and awoke to discover that his body had somehow become bonded with the sand. He had become a living sandman.

SHIFTING SANDS
The Sandman can convert all or part of his body into sand and mold himself into any shape. His mind control is so precise that he can even assume multiple configurations at the same time. His fists can become sledgehammers while his head transforms into a battering ram. He can also fire his sand particles so that they strike his target with the force of hailstones.

The Sandman's mind is in control at all times, even when his head has been turned into sand or exploded by an enemy's fist.

CRYSTALLIZED FURY
The Sandman conned the Hulk into helping him steal a spaceship from General Ross's base. When Betty Ross got in the Sandman's way, the Hulk realized the Sandman would hurt her, and attacked. Baker was thrown into a pressurized vat that caused his sandy body to mutate into crystal.

The Sandman can remain in sand form as long as he likes and there seems to be no limit to how far or how thin he can stretch himself.

A RETALIATORY REMEDY

Realizing that the slightest blow would smash him in pieces, Baker became desperate to find a cure. He learned of a doctor who had perfected a method of completely replacing one person's blood with another's and took him hostage. To get his revenge on the Hulk, Baker chose Betty as his unwilling donor. The Sandman regained his powers after the operation, but Betty was transformed into a lifeless glass statue. She remained trapped in that state until Doc Samson devised a remedy.

THE MISSING LINK

"MEANWHILE, A TEAM OF MILITARY SCIENTISTS WAS SENT OUT TO CAPTURE THE BRUTE...WHICH APPARENTLY HAD SURVIVED IN SUSPENDED ANIMATION FOR COUNTLESS AGES, TO BE REVIVED BY THE BLAST..."

THERE HE IS!

IT'S UNBELIEVABLE! EVOLUTION'S MISSING LINK...ALIVE!

AND, WE MUST KEEP HIM THAT WAY! FIRE YOUR GAS PELLETS!

"SOON, SUBJECTED TO A SERIES OF TESTS, THE SEMI-HUMAN CREATURE BEGAN TO CHANGE IN APPEARANCE...TO THE AMAZEMENT OF THE SCIENTISTS..."

LOOK! THE APELIKE HAIR WHICH COVERED HIS BODY...IT'S FALLING OUT!

AND...WHAT ARE THOSE WEIRD CRYSTALS APPEARING ON HIM?

THIS IS NOT...GREEN ONE WHO ATTACKED ME!

PINK-SKINNED ONE...NOT WORTHY OF BATTLE!

:UHNNN!

RAY REVERSAL
The Missing Link's body is like a living atomic pile that can generate the heat of a miniature sun. His radiation can combine with the Hulk's gamma rays and transform him back into Bruce Banner.

HE NEVER HAD A REAL NAME. None of his friends did, either. He was born many thousands of years ago, long before the idea of naming individuals had become fashionable. He was just one of the numerous near-human Neanderthals who once populated this planet. Life was harsh in that era. Huge monsters still walked the Earth, and it was a constant struggle for survival. He was hunting one day when the ground suddenly shook. A nearby volcano erupted, blasting its seething magma into the air. Trapped by the flowing lava, he thought he was about to die. He was wrong. Like a fly in amber, he became encased within the cooling volcanic rock and fell into a state of suspended animation.

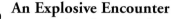

"AND THEN, BEFORE THEIR AMAZED EYES, HE SEEMED SUDDENLY TRANSFORMED BY THE NAMELESS CRYSTALS INTO A GLOWING, PULSATING ENGINE OF DESTRUCTION..."

"NO LONGER WAS HE A PRIMITIVE MISSING LINK... BUT A RADIO-ACTIVE MONSTER, SUCH AS HAD NEVER BEFORE WALKED THE EARTH..."

An Explosive Encounter
An atom bomb test awakened the Missing Link from centuries of slumber, and he began to mutate as radioactive crystals formed on his body. Unable to communicate, he became embroiled in a battle with the Hulk, whose punishing blows shattered the beast-man's crystalline body. As it fused back together, his body released more and more radiation until the Missing Link finally exploded like a bomb.

I AM HOME... MRS. BRICK-FORD!

MONSTER MINER
Unknown to the Hulk, the Missing Link's crystal fragments fell to the Earth. Eventually they reformed and the Missing Link was reborn. He was found by the poor, warmhearted Brickford family, who took him in, tutored him, got him a job at the local coal mine and called him Lincoln, the first name he had ever been given.

HAPPILY EVER AFTER

Life was good for Lincoln until Bruce Banner discovered that Lincoln's radiation was poisoning the town. During another fight with the Hulk, Lincoln reached critical mass and expelled his radiation in a cataclysmic blast. To the Hulk's surprise, the townspeople rushed to Lincoln's aid. The Missing Link had found the true friendship that would always be denied the Hulk.

Violent blows can damage his crystal-like body, but the Missing Link is virtually indestructible because his wounds heal in an instant.

THE GLOB

IF THE SPIRIT'S WILLING
According to an Everglades legend, a man can live forever if he falls into the swamp's embrace and his desire to survive is stronger than the call of the grave.

THERE ARE SOME THINGS science cannot describe; things like the Glob. Joe Timms was once a petty criminal who loved his wife. After being arrested and jailed, he learned that she was dying. Desperate to be reunited with her, he sought an early release. When this was denied, he escaped. Joe fled into the Florida Everglades to elude his pursuers. Lost and alone, he stumbled into a treacherous bog and was sucked under. A few decades later, the Hulk accidentally dumped radioactive waste into the Everglades. The toxic chemicals mixed with the ageless swamp and the restless ghost of Joe Timms to form a marsh-like monster called the Glob.

UNFINISHED BUSINESS
Without realizing it, the Hulk contaminated the swamp that held the body of Joe Timms with radioactive waste. A few hours later a semi-solid mass of slime and bog matter emerged from the stagnant waters with only one desire: to be reunited with Joe's wife.

The Final Sacrifice

The Glob came upon Betty Ross and mistook her for the wife who had died so many years ago. The Hulk tried to rescue Betty but even his strongest blows had no effect. They merely sank into the muck that was the creature's body. When the Glob returned to the swamp, it began to dissolve and somehow realized that the radioactive water would harm Betty. The creature's final act was to hold Betty high above its head so that the Hulk could save her.

RESURRECTED

The Leader came to believe that the Glob might be the only creature mighty enough to destroy the incredible Hulk. Using a special machine he recreated the muck monster and then sent it after the greenskinned giant. Since the Glob could not feel pain and was far stronger, the only way the Hulk could defeat the creature was to hurl it into an experimental dynamo that blew it into millions of tiny particles.

The Everlasting Glob

The tiny particles eventually coalesced. This time, however, the creature helped the Hulk. An alien collector had managed to capture both of them, intending to exhibit them in outer space. The Glob oozed through its bonds and provided a diversion that allowed the Hulk to escape. A second Glob-like creature appeared some years later and was incinerated by the Hulk but witnesses report that the original Glob still haunts the Everglades.

HULK IN THE 1970s

AS THE 1970s BEGAN, Roy Thomas and Harry Herb Trimpe revved up the series with a storyline that guest-starred the Fantastic Four and gave Bruce Banner the ability to control his transformations and retain his intelligence while the Hulk. Bruce immediately proposed to Betty Ross. However, their wedding was spoiled by the Leader and the Rhino. Doctor Strange, the Avengers, and Iron Man made brief appearances, and Jim Wilson became the Hulk's new sidekick. After being convinced that Bruce Banner was dead, Betty Ross married his rival, Glenn Talbot.

The world-famous author Harlan Ellison contributed a story (scripted by Roy), entitled "The Brute That Shouted Love From the Heart of the Atom," that introduced Hulk fans to the warrior-queen Jarella.

Promoted to Marvel's editor-in-chief, Roy Thomas, was replaced by top writers such as Gerry Conway, Archie Goodwin, Steve Englehart, Steve Gerber, Chris Claremont, and Tony Isabella. Len Wein eventually became the Hulk's regular scribe and teamed up with Herb Trimpe to introduce Wolverine, one of the most popular comic-book characters. Len also penned the story that depicted the death of Jarella. Toward the end of 1975, Herb Trimpe moved on and the Hulk's artistic duties became the responsibility of Sal Buscema for nearly ten years.

The Incredible Hulk #123 *(Jan. 1970): Bruce Banner gains control of the Hulk. (Cover by Herb Trimpe)*

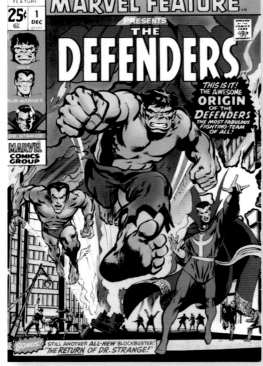

Marvel Feature #1 *(Dec. 1971): The first appearance of the Defenders. (Cover by Ross Andru)*

The biggest news for Hulk fans occurred in 1977 when he appeared in two full-length television movies. Starring Bill Bixby as David (instead of Bruce) Banner and Lou Ferrigno as the Hulk, these films launched a major television series that lasted until 1982. Although the show didn't follow the comic books, it did evoke the Hulk's true character and is still remembered fondly today.

To capitalize on the Hulk's increased popularity, Marvel launched a new magazine called *The Rampaging Hulk*. Aimed at people who only knew the character from television, it featured the talents of such comic book luminaries as Doug Moench, Walt Simonson, Jim Starlin, Alfredo Alcala, Alex Nino, Keith Pollard and Ron Wilson. Roger Stern joined Sal on the Hulk's main title for the decade's final two years. They introduced Fred Sloan and Moonstone, and Doc Samson's first attempts to psychoanalyze the Hulk.

1970

The Incredible Hulk #131 *(Sept. 1970): The invincible Iron Man guest-stars. (Cover by Herb Trimpe)*

1971

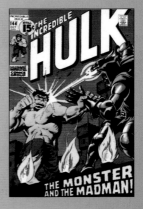

The Incredible Hulk #144 *(Oct. 1971): The Hulk faces Doctor Doom. (Cover by Dick Ayers and John Severin)*

1974

The Incredible Hulk #181 *(Nov. 1974): The first appearance of Wolverine. (Cover by Herb Trimpe)*

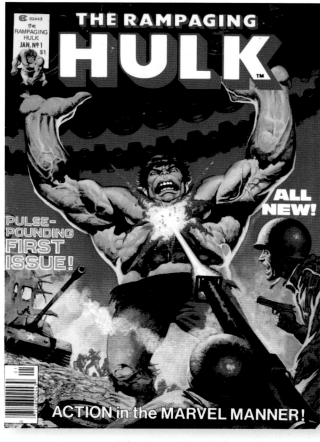

The Rampaging Hulk #1 *(Jan. 1977)*
The Hulk is awarded a second title.
(Painting by Ken Barr)

The Incredible Hulk #200 *(June
1976): Friends and enemies gather
to celebrate the Hulk's 200th issue.
(Cover by Rich Buckler and
John Romita)*

1976

The Incredible
Hulk Annual #5
*(1976): monsters
from Marvel's old
titles gather to fight
the Hulk. (Cover by
Sal Buscema)*

1978

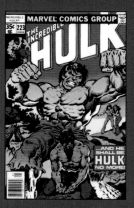

The Incredible
Hulk #223 *(May
1978): Banner is
temporarily cured.
(Cover by Validar
and Ernie Chan)*

1979

Spider-Man Vs.
The Hulk *(1979):
This promotional
comic book was
inserted into
newspapers. (Cover
by John Romita)*

THE DEFENDERS ™

MAGICAL ALLIANCE
Dr. Strange had recently helped Namor battle a band of demons. Realizing that he owed the sorcerer his life, the Sub-Mariner was happy to team up with his old friend.

THE EARTH WAS in grave danger. Doctor Stephen Strange, sorcerer supreme, received an urgent mystical summons. A scientist from another dimension had combined magic with alien technology to create a doomsday device that could explode every nuclear stockpile on the planet! Realizing he lacked the raw physical power needed to destroy this machine, Dr. Strange sought the aid of two former allies: Prince Namor, the Sub-Mariner, and the Hulk. After running a gauntlet of magical and physical deathtraps, the three heroes combined their powers to defend the world from destruction. Strange called on his new friends again when a demon invaded the Earth. As time passed, the three defenders met more often and were joined by the Silver Surfer and the Valkyrie.

FOLLOW THAT GHOST
Dr. Strange was surprised to discover that the Hulk could perceive him while he was in his astral form. The magician had a great respect for the Hulk's strength and loyalty, but often had to taunt him in order to secure his help.

THE TEAM THAT WASN'T!

The Defenders evolved into a loose band of super heroes that sporadically met to battle a common foe. Doctor Strange usually brought the group together, and his *sanctum sanctorum* in New York's Greenwich Village became their unofficial headquarters for a time. The Defenders never had a fixed roster. Anyone who helped them on a mission was considered to be a member and their ranks included super-powered adventurers like the Silver Surfer, the Valkyrie, Nighthawk, Hellcat, the Beast, the Angel, Iceman, and the Gargoyle.

Friends to Fight for
For someone who has always claimed that he just wants to be left alone, the Hulk spent a lot of time with the Defenders. He rarely understood who, what, or why he was fighting, but he didn't care. The other members were outsiders, like him, and he valued their companionship.

Prince Namor, the Sub-Mariner, is the leader of an undersea race from the legendary city of Atlantis.

Almost as strong as the Hulk, he can fly thanks to wings on his feet.

The Silver Surfer, sentinel of space, can manipulate his cosmic energy to become even stronger than the Hulk.

SECRET WARRIORS
Long after the original Defenders disbanded, whenever Doctor Strange saw the need to gather a team of heroes, he would rely on his subconscious mind and an enchanted deck of tarot cards to choose the best heroes to handle each new problem. Those chosen would then go their separate ways after the job was completed.

From Asgard, home of the Norse gods, the Valkyrie is a superb warrior and rides a winged steed.

Dr. Strange is the greatest and most learned magician on Earth.

Cursed to Be Together
The Hulk, Namor, Dr. Strange, and the Silver Surfer were forced to reunite a few years later when one of the Defenders' oldest enemies returned to menace Earth. After seeing how much the former teammates disliked each other, their foe cast a magic spell on them. No matter what they were doing, they were cursed to be drawn together whenever the world was in danger.

The Best Defense
Doomed to be the Earth's champions, the Defenders decided to seize control of the planet and establish a new world order. Each nation was placed on notice. No longer would international crime, war, or pollution be tolerated. The Defenders banned nuclear power, drilling for oil, and animal testing, and they also shut down all entertainment companies because they thought that violent comics, movies, and television shows were bad for people. Outraged by these actions, nearly every super hero on the Earth banded together against the Defenders.

THE PRICE OF FREEDOM
Doctor Strange realized the Defenders were being manipulated by an old foe and brought the planet to the brink of a crisis to free them from their curse.

XEMNU™

THE RULER OF A DISTANT ALIEN PLANET, Xemnu the Titan often warred with his neighbors on other worlds. After being captured and sent to a prison planet on the edge of the Milky Way, he escaped and headed toward the Earth. He temporarily placed the entire world's population under hypnotic control but was expelled back into space. He returned to his home world, only to discover that it had been wiped out by a deadly plague. Desperate to repopulate his planet, he journeyed back to Earth where he began to appear on a children's television program called "Xemnu of the Magic Planet". His show became very popular because he was secretly hypnotizing his young audience; he planned to take them back to his world. The Defenders rescued the kidnapped children and the Hulk overpowered Xemnu.

Xemnu can project mento-blasts of pure concussive force.

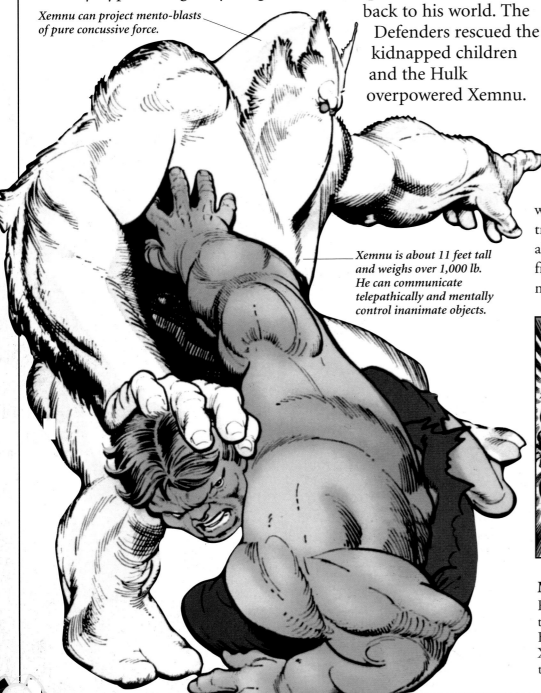

Xemnu is about 11 feet tall and weighs over 1,000 lb. He can communicate telepathically and mentally control inanimate objects.

THE TITAN STRIKES BACK

A few months later Xemnu hypnotized everyone in an isolated village in Florida. He made them build a spaceship to carry them all back to his world. He captured the Hulk and used him as bait to trap the other Defenders. As Xemnu ordered his slaves aboard the spaceship, Doctor Strange cast a spell that freed Hulk from his trance. Xemnu soon learned why no one likes the Hulk when he is angry.

Monsters' Ball

Furious with the Hulk for ruining his plans, Xemnu gathered a team of alien monsters and ordered them to destroy him. The Hulk beating each one, and still had the strength left to resist Xemnu's strongest mento-blasts in a battle that ended when the titan was swept away by a raging flood.

GREMLIN™

TEEN TERROR
For reasons of his own, the Gremlin deliberately lied to the Hulk about his true age and about being born after his father's death.

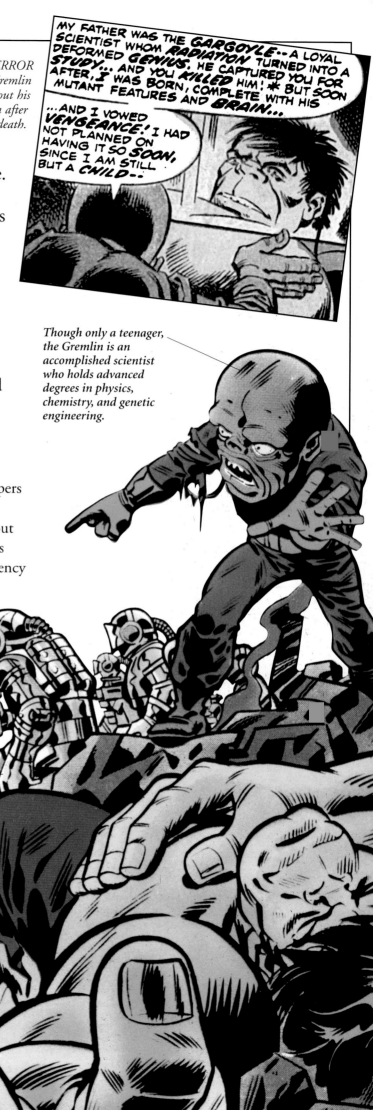

MY FATHER WAS THE *GARGOYLE*-- A LOYAL *SCIENTIST* WHOM *RADIATION* TURNED INTO A DEFORMED *GENIUS*. HE CAPTURED YOU FOR *STUDY*... AND YOU *KILLED* HIM! ✱ BUT SOON AFTER, *I* WAS BORN, COMPLETE WITH HIS MUTANT FEATURES AND *BRAIN*...

...AND I VOWED *VENGEANCE!* I HAD NOT PLANNED ON HAVING IT SO *SOON*, SINCE I AM STILL BUT A *CHILD*--

HE WAS THE SON OF THE GARGOYLE, the Hulk's first super-foe. Born with a mutant brain because of his father's exposure to radiation, the Gremlin grew up in a Siberian hospital, where scientists studied the boy genius. By the time he was 12 years old, the Gremlin had begun to study the scientists and he became their leader before his 15th birthday. Learning that his father had been killed in a battle with the Hulk, the teenager made plans for revenge. In exchange for his promise to design super-weapons, the Russian government gave him a secret laboratory in the Arctic. The Gremlin conceived of an advanced exoskeleton that could give a normal soldier superhuman strength and convinced his superiors that he needed the Hulk to complete his research.

Though only a teenager, the Gremlin is an accomplished scientist who holds advanced degrees in physics, chemistry, and genetic engineering.

MIND OVER MAYHEM

The Gremlin sent a team of his new Super-Troopers to capture the Hulk. The armored men quickly found their target, and sedated him with knockout gas. The Gremlin immediately began to study his prisoner with an eye toward improving the efficiency of his mobile combat suits. The Hulk escaped, but later returned when the Gremlin attempted to use Glenn Talbot in a plot to assassinate the President of the United States. The Gremlin then tried to brainwash the Hulk using an experimental device called the Psi-Clone, but the Greenskinned Giant's mind was too primitive for the procedure to work.

The Gremlin's elite Super-Troopers were bio-engineered to become the perfect blend of man and machine.

"GENTLY! GENTLY NOW," THE GREMLIN'S VOICE IS STRANGELY *DEEP* FOR ONE SO YOUNG. "LOWER THE BRUTE INTO THE *PSI-PHON* GENTLY!"

I WILL *DECAPITATE* THE FIRST COMRADE WHO *DISRUPTS* THIS DELICATE STAGE OF THE PROCEEDINGS!

The Titanium Teen
The Gremlin built himself an armored battle suit powerful enough to rival the one worn by Iron Man. The Gremlin now possessed enough strength to challenge the Hulk, but never got the chance. He was killed while battling Iron Man. However, since his body was never recovered, there may *still* be a Gremlin in the works!

Jarella was a great warrior, a just empress, and a brilliant military leader.

JARELLA™

LOVE AT FIRST SIGHT
Jarella was immediately attracted to the Hulk. She commanded her sorcerers to cast a spell that taught him their language and also had the side effect of giving him the intelligence of Bruce Banner.

MANY WOMEN have been attracted to Bruce Banner over the years, but only one has ever loved the Hulk. Her name was Jarella, and she was the empress of K'ai, a city-state in another dimension. Jarella assumed the throne shortly after her 17th summer when her father died beneath an assassin's blade. On her 21st birthday, the Pantheon of Sorcerers declared that it was time for her to marry. They required her to wed a warrior who had proven himself in battle against the warthos, an enormous warthog-like beast that roamed the countryside. No one had defeated even a *single* warthos, until one day a stranger appeared and conquered an entire pack! That stranger was the Hulk, who had been transported to K'ai by a super-villain named Psyklop. Though the Hulk missed his true love, Betty Ross, he was very happy in K'ai. He also grew to care for Jarella and agreed to become her husband. However, on the eve of their wedding, Psyklop brought the Hulk back to Earth.

THE EMERALD QUEEN'S ANSWER IS ELOQUENT *SILENCE.* THE MAGIC BEGINS..

A BRIEF REUNION
Civil war broke out in K'ai, but Jarella was still brokenhearted over the loss of the Hulk. She begged the Pantheon of Sorcerers to help her find him. They sent her to Earth, but an assassin followed her. The Hulk captured this executioner, but Jarella realized that her people needed her and sadly returned to K'ai.

She was an excellent swordswoman and skilled in hand-to-hand combat.

TIME IS *VANISHING.* CAN YOU COMPREHEND, TRY TO SEE....?

HULK SEES YOU WANT TO TAKE ONLY *GOOD THING* IN HIS LIFE.'

DON'T *CARE* ABOUT THE SUN...THE WORLD...ONLY *JARELLA!*

TOUCH HER AND SEE HOW FAST THE HULK CAN *SMASH!*

GREENSKINNED GUARDIAN
The Hulk truly came to love Jarella. He was very protective and would smash anyone who dared to threaten her. He was even willing to forsake Earth and spend the rest of his life in K'ai just to be with her.

RAVAGED BY REVOLUTION

The Hulk returned to K'ai, only to discover that the city was in ruins and that Jarella was missing. Her cousin, Lord Visis, the leader of the rebel forces, had taken Jarella hostage and threatened to kill all her loyal subjects if she didn't agree to marry him. By leading a pack of wild warthos against Visis's stronghold, the Hulk created enough confusion to rescue Jarella and free her people. With the Hulk leading her army, the revolt was soon crushed, and so was Visis.

There, Hulk—do you see? The legends are all true!

Before us stands the castle of the mountain god!

Bah! Looks like big rock with windows to Hulk!

But if that is where Hulk will find mountain god, then that is where Hulk will go!

Lair of the Mountain God

The next time the Hulk went to K'ai, he arrived barely in time to prevent Jarella from being sacrificed to a mountain god who was ravaging her world with earthquakes. The Hulk and Jarella sneaked into the mountain god's castle and learned that he was actually a giant robot that had been built and programmed by Psyklop.

Blood in rivers running deep—who dares invade my castle keep?

H-He lies so solemn—so still! By the all the gods, I cannot have found my one true love again, only to have led him to his death!

Hulk? Hulk?? I beg you, my love—please speak to me!

You are wasting your breath, woman. The man-brute cannot hear you—which is, in it's fashion, a pity!

You wanted to know who constructed the god of the mountain, and now you have your answer--but it will avail you nothing!

For nothing that lives can hope to stand before the power of—Psyklop!

PSYKLOP'S REVENGE
Determined to conquer Jarella's world, Psyklop had secretly caused the earthquakes. He also hypnotized the Hulk and sent him against Jarella's people. But the Hulk broke free of his control and overpowered Psyklop. Now her people were safe, Jarella decided to marry the Hulk and live on his world.

Insect Revival

Psyklop is the last survivor of an ancient insect-like race that once inhabited the Earth. His people lived far below the planet's surface and became extinct long before the coming of humanity. Awakened after thousands of years in suspended animation, Psyklop vowed to revive the rest of his race and to retake the Earth.

On her homeworld, the woman called Jarella had been a queen. The lives of countless beings were her responsibility—and hers alone.

It seems that some habits are unfortunately hard to break!

UNHAPPY ENDING
One day, Bruce Banner and Jarella were enjoying a quiet walk when a robot attempted to rob a nearby bank. While the Hulk battled the robot, a falling chunk of debris endangered a small boy and Jarella heroically sacrificed herself to save him. The Hulk refused to accept her death for many months and he is still haunted by memories of Jarella.

Jarella?

--But the jade-skinned Jar-ella does not fare nearly as well!

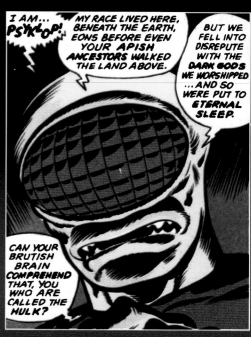

I am... Psyklop!

My race lived here, beneath the earth, eons before even your apish ancestors walked the land above.

But we fell into disrepute with the dark gods we worshipped ...and so were put to eternal sleep.

Can your brutish brain comprehend that, you who are called the Hulk?

Seeking to exploit the Hulk's strength, Psyklop attempted to study him by compressing his atomic structure.

DOCTOR SAMSON

After being exposed to gamma rays, Dr. Leonard Samson grew nearly 8 in and gained almost 200 lb of bone and muscle.

DR. LEONARD SAMSON and Dr. Bruce Banner had a lot in common. Both were medical students of average build who were exposed to enormous doses of radiation. And both ended up as massively muscled, green-haired superhumans. However, that's where the similarities end. Bruce was never interested in athletics or physical activity. Leonard was a born competitor who played team sports and enjoyed skiing and scuba diving. Bruce left medical school to become a nuclear physicist. Leonard became a renowned psychiatrist. Bruce tried to harness the power of gamma radiation for destruction. Leonard believed that gamma rays could be used to heal the mentally ill. Bruce wanted the quiet life of a scientist and became the Hulk by accident. Leonard dreamed of being a super hero and deliberately exposed himself to gamma radiation.

TO SAVE BETTY
To test his theories on gamma rays' healing powers, Dr. Samson approached General Ross after learning that the general's daughter had been transformed into a crystal-like creature by the Sandman and was about to die. Aided by Bruce Banner, Samson built a machine that drained gamma radiation from the Hulk. This energy was used to cure Betty Ross.

BIRTH OF A HERO
After saving Betty, Samson noticed that his machine still held plenty of the Hulk's energy. To see how a controlled burst of gamma radiation would affect a normal human, Samson exposed himself to the rays. His body bulked up as it gained the power of the Hulk and his hair turned green. Dr. Leonard Samson was now Doc Samson!

Being a psychiatrist, Samson can predict how Hulk will react and prepare an appropriate defense.

STAYING IN SHAPE

Though almost as strong as the Hulk, Doc Samson still possesses a mind as sharp as a scalpel. In many ways, he is the perfect combination of mind and body. Gamma radiation enhanced his cellular structure, fortified his skeleton, and added a few hundred pounds of muscle to his body, but Samson exercises every day in order to keep in peak physical condition. Realizing that he needs more than strength and stamina, he follows a strict program designed to increase his speed and agility.

YOU SEE, I'VE BEEN *EXPERIMENTING* ON MYSELF-- EVER SINCE I SIPHONED OFF SOME OF THE *HULK'S STRENGTH.*

I LEARNED THAT, IN SOME UNCANNY WAY, JUST LIKE THE *ORIGINAL SAMSON* --

--MY *RAW POWER* VARIED DIRECTLY WITH THE LENGTH OF THIS *GREEN HAIR* THE GAMMA RAYS GAVE ME.

IN POINT OF FACT, I FOUND IT INCREASINGLY HARD TO *CONTROL* MY STRENGTH---

--TILL I TOOK SCISSORS IN HAND, AND PLAYED MY OWN *DELILAH.*

THE HAIRY HERO
Like his biblical namesake, Doc Samson eventually discovered that his power is somehow connected to the length of his hair. His strength decreases when his hair is cut and increases as it grows. Since his hair has a tendency to get in his way when it grows too long, Samson never allows it to grow beyond a certain length.

The Hulk's Analyst
Doc Samson has used his medical training to try to help the Hulk. He believes Bruce Banner's exposure to gamma radiation has saddled him with a terrible curse. After analyzing Bruce's dreams, Samson realized that the Hulk and Bruce Banner were not just two different sides of the same mind, but separate beings who were constantly at war within the one body. Samson devised a plan to physically separate Banner from the Hulk, but later realized that it would be better to integrate the warring factions into a single, united personality.

WELCOME, GENTLEMEN, TO SOME GENUINE UNREAL ESTATE: THE MIND OF BRUCE BANNER.

I SUPPOSE YOU'RE WONDERING WHY I'VE CALLED YOU ALL HERE.

MIND OVER MUSCLE
Doc Samson may be the physical equal of a relaxed Hulk, but he cannot match the untamed savagery of an angry one. Since the Hulk grows stronger as he gets angrier, Samson has to find ways to keep the greenskinned Goliath calm. Samson's mind is his greatest asset in any battle with the Hulk.

--HIT 'EM! HARD AND FAST!

THE GREEN TEAM
Doc Samson and the Hulk have worked together almost as often as they have battled each other. They once teamed up against the Leader who used his Humanoids to seize control of Gamma Base. Samson has often risked his life to defend the Hulk, and he has never stopped trying to find a cure for Bruce Banner.

Samson's Sidekick
When Doc Samson was hired as a profiler in the hunt for a gamma-irradiated serial killer who was stalking the streets of New York City, he met a young university student known as Geiger. She had been exposed to a particle accelerator and gained the ability to latch onto nearby radiation patterns and copy them. Naturally, she used her new powers to become a female version of Doc Samson.

THE ABSURBING MAN™

> YOU *GOT* IT, SUCKER! AN' NOW THAT I'M IN CLOSE *CONTACT* WITH YA, I'M STARTING TA *ABSORB* ALL OF YER *STRENGTH*--

> ALMOST BLEW MY *COOL* A MINNIT AGO, GRUESOME!

> BUT, SOON AS I REMEMBERED *WHO* I WUZ...AND *WHAT* I WUZ...

> I KNEW THE IMPACT WOULD ONLY TURN ME INTO...*SOLID STONE*!

> NOW GET READY TO MEET YER *MAKER*... 'CAUSE IT'S TIME FOR THE *FINAL ROUND*!!

CARL "CRUSHER" CREEL was a brutal leg-breaker who spent must of his life behind bars. He was in jail for assault when Loki, the Norse god of mischief, decided to use him as a pawn against the mighty Thor. After whipping up a magic potion that gave Crusher the ability to absorb the physical properties of anything he touched, Loki arranged for him to fight Thor. The Absorbing Man was defeated while helping Loki conquer Asgard, home of the Norse gods. Exiled in outer space, Crusher returned to Earth by hitching a ride on a comet, and that's when he first ran into the Hulk.

Clash on a Comet
The military observed the Absorbing Man's comet as it approached the Earth. Fearing that it might poison the planet's atmosphere, they sent Bruce Banner in an experimental rocket to destroy it. Crusher leaped aboard the scientist's ship at the last minute and attacked the cockpit, forcing Banner to transform into the Hulk.

STICKS AND STONES
It doesn't pay to hurl objects or use weapons against the Absorbing Man because he can duplicate any material the instant it touches him.

The Absorbing Man retains his intelligence when he changes form and he can reassemble himself if his body is broken.

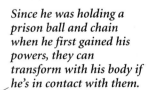

THIS MAN IS AN ISLAND
Contacted by a group that wanted the Hulk dead, Crusher later attacked Bruce Banner on a construction site but was defeated when he accidentally turned himself into glass. He also battled the Hulk on Easter Island where he soaked up the properties of the very ground and eventually transformed himself into a small island!

Since he was holding a prison ball and chain when he first gained his powers, they can transform with his body if he's in contact with them.

> ...BUT HULK IS GOING TO *FIND OUT*!

> WITH HULK'S *BARE HANDS*, HULK WILL *SMASH* YOU INTO...

> AARRGGNH!!

> YA BRAINLESS *BABOON* -- MY SKIN IS ALMOST *MOLTEN*!

VEGAS VENGEANCE

A gangster offered Creel $1 million to kill casino owner Michael Berengetti and his bodyguard Joe Fixit. Crusher learned that Fixit was the Hulk in disguise and chased him to the top of Hoover Dam. Absorbing a generator, Crusher tried to electrocute the Hulk but short-circuited when his ball and chain hit the water. Crusher turned into concrete, but the Hulk shattered him and tossed the pieces into the Colorado River. Later, Creel married his girlfriend Titania, but still commits the occasional crime.

THE JUGGERNAUT™

SPOILED BY A DOTING FATHER, Cain Marko bullied anyone who got in his way and took whatever he wanted. While in Korea, he found an ancient idol inside a ruined temple. On the idol's lap was a ruby with the inscription, "Whosoever touches this gem shall possess the power of the Crimson Bands of Cyttorak. Henceforth, you who read these words shall become forevermore a human juggernaut." Cain seized the ruby and was transformed into the Juggernaut. He gained super-strength and became virtually indestructible. Though he usually focuses his hatred on his half-brother, Charles Xavier, leader of the X-Men, the Juggernaut has also battled the Hulk. No one can stop the Juggernaut, but the Hulk slammed him into a mountain hard enough to jar his helmet loose.

His helmet shields him from psionic attacks and he can generate a force field that protects him from physical harm.

Amazon Adventure

While working for the Pantheon, the Hulk learned that someone was leveling acres of rainforest and went to investigate. A super-strong construction worker—the Juggernaut without his armor—attacked the Hulk and knocked him unconscious. Taking control of the Hulk's mind, Marko sent him against the Avengers. The Hulk eventually regained his senses, causing a psychic backlash that flattened the Juggernaut.

Once the Juggernaut is in motion, no physical force or obstacle can halt his progress.

BITTER RIVALS
Though the Juggernaut is the hypothetical "irresistible force", the Hulk is the equally theoretical "immovable object". No matter how many times they have battled, neither has ever won a decisive victory over the other. They are just too evenly matched.

OOOOOOFF!

PAWN OF APOCALYPSE

The Juggernaut later learned that the Hulk had been recruited by a mutant called Apocalypse who dreamed of conquering the world. A seemingly immortal, super-strong shapeshifter, Apocalypse brainwashed the Hulk and temporarily increased his power. Frustrated by his previous failures, the Juggernaut formed a brief partnership with the Absorbing Man, but even their combined power wasn't enough to beat the new Hulk. Undaunted, Cain Marko still believes that he'll eventually find a way to conquer the Hulk because nothing can stop the Juggernaut.

THE SHAPER OF WORLDS

THE SHAPER OF WORLDS is a machine created by an alien race called the Skrulls. Used by the race's emperor, this device appeared to have the ability to reshape reality and it was quite similar to an earthly creation called the Cosmic Cube. It developed a mind of its own and eventually journeyed to Earth. The Shaper first fell afoul of the Hulk when it chose to fulfill the fantasies of an ex-Nazi scientist and create a micro-dimension in which the Nazis had won World War II. The Shaper tried to force the Hulk to accept this fantasy—without success. The Shaper can create lifelike fantasies, but relies on others to supply it with dreams. The Shaper can teleport anywhere in the universe.

From the waist down, the Shaper's torso is completely robotic and he travels on tractor treads.

The Shaper of Worlds was created to make dreams come true and that is its only source of pleasure.

The Shaper only appears to be wearing armor. The metal that covers his chest is actually the outer shell of his artificial body.

DREAMWEAVER
A vastly powerful empath, the Shaper of Worlds sees the images in a person's mind and duplicates them. The Shaper doesn't really create new worlds. It merely reshapes the molecules of an existing planet or dimension to fit the dream. A fantasy can last as long as the Shaper chooses.

PARADISE LOST

Feeling guilty for the way it first treated the Hulk, the Shaper of Worlds secretly sent Glorian to visit the green giant and lead him to a place he could call home. It was a land of eternal peace and enchantment where the Hulk was no longer an outsider and where he found his dead friends Crackerjack Jackson and Jarella waiting for him. The Hulk might have stayed on this world forever, but invading aliens ruined everything when they disrupted the Shaper's illusions.

Glorian
Thomas Gideon was a young man who developed radiation poisoning in trying to gain super-powers. Fearing he would not survive to fulfill his dreams, Gideon agreed to become the Shaper of Worlds' apprentice. He was transformed into Glorian and used his imagination to craft fantasies full of peace and contentment.

WENDIGO™

A GREAT BEAST STALKS the Canadian North Woods, a monster that was once a man. According to legend, an ancient curse befalls anyone who eats human flesh. The cannibal loses all trace of humanity as his body mutates into a 10-ft-tall creature known as a Wendigo. While in northern Canada, the Hulk learned that three hunters had been attacked by a wolf pack and had sought shelter in a cave. Trapped for nearly a week without food and water, one of the hunters died and another did the unspeakable and became a Wendigo. After rescuing the third hunter, the Hulk tried to capture the creature and restore its humanity. But not even the Hulk could defeat the curse of the Wendigo.

THE ETERNAL SAVAGE
The Wendigo is so fearsome that even the Hulk considers it a monster. It is much stronger than the Hulk and is impervious to pain or injury. The creature's magical nature makes it virtually impossible to kill, and it never grows old.

Watch Out for Wolverine
The Wendigo's sister tried to transfer the curse from her brother to someone else. She chose the Hulk, figuring that the curse couldn't be any worse than the one he already had. She used magic to summon the Hulk, drugged him, and was about to perform the magical ceremony when Wolverine intervened.

AND SASQUATCH MAKES THREE
Bruce Banner was journeying through Canada a few months later when he stumbled upon a cabin that belonged to the Wendigo. Changing into the Hulk, he was joined by Sasquatch and the two gamma-spawned gladiators teamed up to apprehend the monster.

Weighing nearly 1,800 lb, the Wendigo has razor-sharp talons and fangs that can bite through solid steel.

THE FERAL FILMMAKER

Desiring the power of the Wendigo, a young filmmaker named Lorenzo began to study all the legends about the creature. He consulted shamans, gypsies, and sorcerers and eventually obtained a mystic talisman that allowed him to retain his intelligence after the transformation. His dreams of controlling the beast's power were shattered when the Hulk teamed up with the new Captain Marvel.

WE MEAN JUST THIS, HUMAN; CREATURES FROM YOUR PALE GREEN PLANET EARTH ARE RESPONSIBLE FOR THE DESTRUCTION OF OUR WORLD!!

THUS WE INTEND TO DESTROY YOUR WORLD IN TURN!!!

DESIRE FOR VENGEANCE
The Bi-Beast believes that the bird-people should have ruled the Earth. He has often attempted to destroy humanity because he wants revenge for driving his people into exile.

BI-BEAST ™

A RACE OF WINGED creatures once lived on Earth. As humankind began to dominate the planet, these bird-like people used their highly advanced technology to build a city in the sky. They disdained contact with other races and lived for thousands of years. Gradually, their civilization began to decay. Realizing they were headed for extinction, the bird-people constructed a monument to their achievements, a living repository for all their knowledge. It was an android with two brains—the Bi-Beast. The upper brain possessed all their technical wisdom and the lower one all their cultural scholarship. Since the machines that kept the sky city afloat were supposed to run forever, the Bi-Beast was never taught how to repair them and needed help when they began to fail.

CALAMITY IN THE CLOUDS

Desperate to fix the damaged machines, the Bi-Beast kidnapped Bruce Banner and Betty Ross. The upper brain wanted to put the scientist to work and the lower brain was attracted to Betty. The Bi-Beast didn't realize that MODOK was following Banner and planning to kill the Hulk. Awed by the wonders of the floating city, MODOK attempted to conquer it. The Bi-Beast destroyed his home rather than let it fall into MODOK's hands.

IN A TIME LONG PAST NOW, A RACE OF WONDROUS BIRD-PEOPLE DWELT UPON A FABULOUS ISLAND IN THE SKY, WHICH WAS HIDDEN BY CLOUDS FROM THE SPINNING WORLD BELOW!

AS THE YEARS WORE ON, THEIR ANCIENT CIVILIZATION DECAYED, AND THEIR RACE BEGAN TO DIE...

"...BUT BEFORE THEY PASSED INTO ETERNAL OBLIVION, THEY CREATED AN ANDROID CREATURE TO SERVE AS A LIVING REPOSITORY OF ALL THEIR ACCUMULATED KNOWLEDGE!

"IN SHORT, THEY CREATED US... THE BI-BEAST!"

ISLAND IN THE SKY
The bird-people built their floating city as a refuge from mankind. It hovered exactly eight miles above the Earth and was perpetually hidden within a cloud.

The Bi-Beast is as strong as the Hulk and as smart as Bruce Banner.

Countdown to Catastrophe
The Bi-Beast soon learned about the S.H.I.E.L.D. Helicarrier, a huge airborne mobile command base for a worldwide intelligence organization. After seizing control of it, the android attacked the Hulk with lasers, but even they couldn't stop the greenskinned giant. The Bi-Beast started capturing ships and melting them down for parts to build a new sky city, but the mighty Thor quickly ended that scheme. The lower skull-brother then became infatuated with the She-Hulk but she didn't return his affections. Though recently defeated by the new Defenders, the Bi-Beast is still at large.

YOU DARED DEFY THE BI-BEAST, HULK-- AND NOW YOU MUST PAY THE PRICE!

EVEN IF THESE POWERFUL LASERS CANNOT PENETRATE YOUR WRETCHED EMERALD SKIN--

--THE OVERWHELMING HEAT THEY GENERATE CAN STILL BOIL THE BLOOD WITHIN YOU!

ZZZAX™

H E MAY LOOK LIKE a mass of electrical sparks, but Zzzax is an intelligent being. He was created by accident when a terrorist group raided a nuclear plant. An exploding generator started a chain reaction that created an electromagnetic field. As the field expanded, it incinerated the terrorists and absorbed the energy in their brains. The more brain power it acquired, the more intelligent Zzzax grew. Hungry for more brainwaves, Zzzax began to attack innocent bystanders and eventually clashed with the Hulk. Zzzax soon found out that he couldn't devour the Hulk's brain energy or reduce him to ashes. They battled until Zzzax was short-circuited by a metal wire that connected him to Manhattan's East River.

DESTROYER FROM THE DYNAMO

Zzzax was accidentally reenergized when some scientists built a machine that collected human brain waves. Freed when the machine exploded, Zzzax kidnapped one of the scientists and climbed atop a building with her during a thunderstorm. The Hulk battled Zzzax until a bolt of lightning overwhelmed the energy creature.

Fury at 50,000 Volts

A few years later, after returning to Earth, Zzzax absorbed the brainwaves of General Ross. Since Ross was obsessed with destroying the Hulk that quickly became Zzzax's top priority. After failing to kill both Bruce Banner and Rick Jones, Zzzax freed himself from Ross's control. His current whereabouts are unknown.

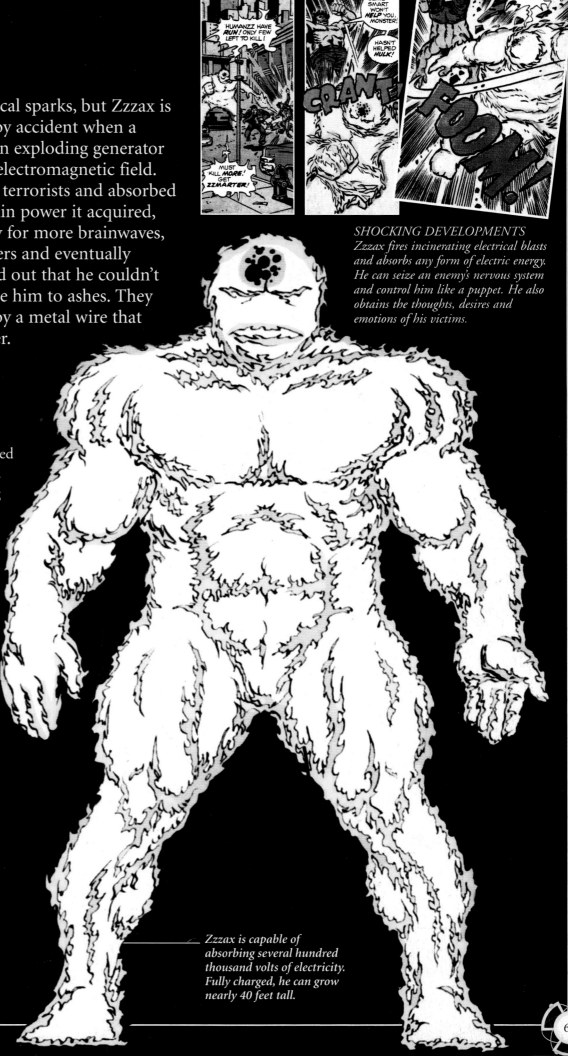

SHOCKING DEVELOPMENTS
Zzzax fires incinerating electrical blasts and absorbs any form of electric energy. He can seize an enemy's nervous system and control him like a puppet. He also obtains the thoughts, desires and emotions of his victims.

Zzzax is capable of absorbing several hundred thousand volts of electricity. Fully charged, he can grow nearly 40 feet tall.

SHE-HULK™

JENNIFER WALTERS always had a wild streak. She was born in Los Angeles, California, where her father was a county sheriff. Jennifer just wanted to have fun, but her dad tried to tame her by setting down stringent rules, which she usually ignored. Whenever she got to be too much for him, he would ship his rebellious daughter off to Dayton, Ohio, to stay with her mother's relatives, the Banners. She looked up to her quiet older cousin Bruce and they became close friends, though they lost touch when they went to college to pursue different careers. While Bruce studied medicine and nuclear physics, Jennifer went to law school and became a defense attorney, much to her father's annoyance.

ATTEMPTED ASSASSINATION

Defending criminals can occasionally be hazardous to one's health. Bruce Banner was visiting Jennifer when she was gunned down before his eyes. Knowing that they possessed the same blood type, he used his medical training to rig an emergency transfusion to save her life. When the assassins later returned to finish their work, Jennifer suddenly transformed into a female version of the Hulk. When she first gained her powers, Jennifer could transform back into her human form by concentrating. She lost this ability when she was exposed to an intense burst of gamma radiation.

UNEXPECTED REACTION
Bruce's gamma-irradiated blood changed Jennifer's life forever! She now had the ability to become a She-Hulk and possessed superhuman strength and durability. Unlike her cousin, however, she retained her courtroom-trained mind and did not grow stronger as she became angrier.

HANG IN THERE, KID! YOU'RE GONNA MAKE IT!

YOU'VE GOTTA MAKE IT!

The She-Hulk stands 6-ft 7-in tall and weighs around 650 lb. Her skin is able to withstand extreme temperatures and is highly resistant to injury.

Although not nearly as strong as the hulk, she can still lift 75 tons without breaking sweat.

NOW LET'S SEE HOW TOUGH YOU ARE--AGAINST ME!

IT'S A GIRL! BUT-- LOOK AT THE SIZE OF HER!

HER SKIN! IT-IT'S GREEN!

IT'S LIKE-- SHE'S SOME KIND'A SHE-HULK!

Career Minded

Jennifer hoped to maintain her defense practice and keep her She-Hulk identity secret, but soon realized that wasn't going to work. She would capture criminals as the She-Hulk and then have to defend them as Jennifer Walters! She decided to become a prosecutor and joined the D.A.'s office in New York. Jennifer still practices law and often represents other super heroes; however, she would much rather stomp a bad guy than sit in a courtroom.

Titania

Mary "Skeeter" MacPherran was a smalltime grifter from Denver, Colorado. Exposed to various radiation treatments, she gained super-strength and took the name Titania. Stronger than She-Hulk but an inch shorter, Titania almost beat Jennifer to death in their first battle. This led to a feud between the two women. Titania started dating the Absorbing Man and eventually married him.

INCARNATIONS
The She-Hulk has gone through changes over the years. She was mutated into a She-Titan when Xemnu chose her for his bride. She turned gray and savage for a time and even switched bodies with her dumpy, middle-aged P.A. But no matter what, Jennifer has never regretted becoming She-Hulk.

TEAM PLAYER
Jennifer works with others a lot better than her cousin. She was invited to join the Avengers and briefly replaced the Thing in the Fantastic Four. She's had far fewer fights with other super heroes, too.

SHE'S THE ONE
Bruce Banner and the Hulk have two distinct personalities but that's not the case with She-Hulk. Other than feeling a little freer to shed her inhibitions, Jennifer and the She-Hulk talk, act, and think the same way.

ABOMINATRIX

Ms. Personality Plus

She claims she's not fat, only big boned. The Abominatrix possesses the strength and physical appearance of the Abomination, and an exceptionally sour disposition. She doesn't like super-heroes in general and the She-Hulk in particular. Aside from soap operas, bon-bons, and landing on her victims from great heights, the Abominatrix doesn't like much. What else would you expect from someone who is the product of a failed medical experiment to control chronic irritability? Abominatrix keeps her real name a secret, probably because she has at least three ex-husbands that she's trying to avoid.

WHEN WOMEN WAR
The Abominatrix came to the She-Hulk's attention when she was hired to kidnap Jennifer's P.A. Though stronger and tougher than the She-Hulk, the Abominatrix prefers watching television to fighting. She used to work as a bank teller, but now earns her living as a bodyguard and an enforcer. The pay is better and she likes her afternoons free so she can catch her favorite soaps.

SASQUATCH™

AN ACT OF WILL
Dr. Walter Langkowski requires intense concentration to change into Sasquatch. This process has grown easier over the years, but is still very painful.

...HIS MUSCLES TENSE AND SWELL...

AND ALL THE WHILE, THE GOLDEN MANE GROWS, THE SKIN DARKENS, AND FINALLY, WALTER LANGKOWSKI LOOKS OUT THROUGH SCARLET-TINTED EYES-

...HIS NAILS STRETCH INTO TALON-LIKE CLAWS!

--AND RISES TO HIS FEET ONCE MORE AS-

BORN AND RAISED in Vancouver, Canada, Walter Langkowski won a football scholarship to Pennsylvania State University. There he met Bruce Banner, who inspired him to study gamma radiation. After graduating, Langkowski continued his studies while pursuing a career in American football. Once it became known that Bruce Banner was the Hulk, Langkowski retired from the game and dedicated himself to gamma research. He gathered information on the Hulk and anyone else who had been transformed by gamma radiation. Hoping to find a cure for Banner, Langkowski designed a machine that generated the same type of gamma rays that had created the Hulk. He used the equipment on himself and was transformed into a 10-foot-tall creature he named Sasquatch. Unlike the Hulk, Langkowski was able to maintain his normal personality and intelligence while in this bestial form.

--SASQUATCH!

Dr. Langkowski has extensive knowledge of physics and is an expert on the effects of radiation.

Former professional athlete Langkowski enjoys being Sasquatch but wishes he was stronger than the Hulk.

CONTEST OF CHAMPIONS

When Langkowski heard that the Hulk had been sighted in British Columbia, he transformed into Sasquatch. Claiming that he merely wanted to learn who was the more powerful for scientific reasons, Langkowski kept his real name a secret and goaded his old friend into a fight. Their battle laid waste to an entire forest and confirmed that the Hulk was truly the strongest one of all.

Alpha Flight
The Canadian Ministry of Defense funded Dr. Langkowski's research in exchange for his participation in Alpha Flight, a team of costumed adventurers with a fluctuating membership. Although the color of his fur has turned from orange to white, Langkowski remains active as Sasquatch.

MOONSTONE™

GUIDED BY A GANGSTER
Karla studied under Doctor Faustus, a master psychiatrist and long-time foe of Captain America. Faustus used his knowledge of psychology to advance his criminal career.

KARLA SOFEN'S FATHER was a butler and her mother was a maid. She was surrounded by great wealth, but wasn't allowed to enjoy it. Karla learned early how to manipulate people. She obtained new clothes from the daughter of her parents' employer by telling the girl that they made her look fat. After Karla's father died, her mother took three jobs to send her to the best schools. Karla studied psychiatry to learn how to control people. Intending to use her skills to become rich and powerful, Dr. Sofen arranged to treat a super-villain called Moonstone. By combining a hallucinogenic gas with her own talents, she brainwashed the man into thinking that the source of his power—an extraterrestrial rock charged with incredible energy—was turning him into a hideous monster.

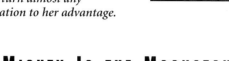

Moonstone's greatest weapon is her mind. She is a master manipulator who can turn almost any situation to her advantage.

A Harsh Mistress
Karla persuaded the original Moonstone to give her the rock. Once it became bonded to her nervous system, she designed a costume for herself and attempted to steal military secrets from General Ross's missile base. The new Moonstone ran into the Hulk and convinced him that everyone hated him. She later cajoled General Ross into suffering a nervous breakdown.

MIGHTY IS THE MOONSTONE

Though nowhere near the Hulk's level, Moonstone possesses superhuman strength, speed, and stamina. She can fly and project laser-like blasts from her hands. She can also generate bursts of blinding light and can phase through solid objects. After encountering heroes like Captain America and Spider-Man, Moonstone joined a group of super-villains called the Masters of Evil and battled the Avengers. Her neck was broken at one point, but her alien rock healed her.

Comes the Thunder
When the Avengers temporarily vanished, the Masters of Evil filled the gap and disguised themselves as heroes. Moonstone adopted a new costume and called herself Meteorite. Now called the Thunderbolts, the new team took on the Hulk. Pretending to be a hero had a positive effect on Karla Sofen. She dated Hawkeye, a former Avenger, and tried to make up for her past crimes.

HULK IN THE 1980s

The Hulk was still rampaging across television screens when the new decade began and Bill Mantlo became his new writer. Hoping to take advantage of the Hulk's popularity, Bill guest-starred other Marvel super stars like Thor and the Silver Surfer and created hordes of new characters. He also sent the Hulk around the world as if to show that the U.S. wasn't the only country with super heroes! The Hulk finally returned Jarella to her home world and witnessed the death of his long time rival Glenn Talbot. Rick Jones rejoined the series and almost died when he deliberately exposed himself to gamma rays. After gaining the intelligence of Bruce Banner, the Hulk won amnesty for his past crimes. No longer hunted by the authorities, it looked as if he was about to live happily ever after when a nightmarish extradimensional creature caused him to revert to a savage monster. With the aid of artists Sal Buscema, Gerry Talaoc, Bret Blevins and Mike Mignola, the Hulk was exiled to the Crossroads of Eternity where he confronted his childhood demons.

Questprobe #1 (Aug. 1984):
The Hulk stars in a new computer game.
(Cover by John Romita)

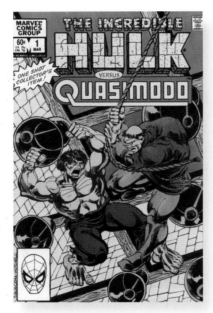

The Incredible Hulk Versus Quasimodo #1 (March 1983): A special adventure designed to promote the Hulk's animated cartoon series. (Cover by Sal Buscema and Steve Mitchell)

Writer-artist John Byrne took over the title for a brief stint, during which Bruce Banner was physically separated from his greenskinned alter ego and he finally married Betty Ross.

Writer Al Milgrom returned the Hulk to his gray-skinned glory after 20 years. Working with artists Dell Barras, Danny Bulanadi, Dennis Janke, and Steve Geiger, Al also recombined Bruce with the Hulk and gave Rick Jones the ability to transform into a Hulk-like creature.

Peter David began a 12-year run as the Hulk's writer by exploring and developing the character of the gray Hulk. With artist Todd McFarlane, Peter brought back the Leader and changed his appearance and agenda. The revamped Samuel Sterns stole a gamma bomb, created some new gamma people, and set up his own personal version of utopia, named Freehold. Artist Jeff Purves joined Peter as the Hulk became a bouncer for a Las Vegas casino and began to call himself Joe Fixit.

As the decade drew to a close, the Hulk returned to television, starring in two movie-length specials: *The Incredible Hulk Returns* (guest-starring the mighty Thor) and *The Trial of the Incredible Hulk* (featuring the first live action version of Daredevil).

1980

'80

The Savage She-Hulk #1 (Feb. 1980): The first appearance of the Hulk's cousin. (Cover by John Buscema)

1982

Hulk #271 (May, 1982): The Hulk marks his 20th year with the debut of Rocket Raccoon. (Cover by Al Milgrom)

1983

Hulk #279 (Jan. 1983): The Hulk is given amnesty and finds acceptance. (Cover by Greg LaRocque)

Hulk #324 *(Oct. 1986):*
A misguided experiment (and
improved printing) allows the
Hulk to become gray again.
(Cover by Al Milgrom after
Jack Kirby)

Hulk Annual #12 *(1983)*
The Hulk learns a terrible lesson.
(Cover by Brent Anderson)

1985

Hulk #311 *(Sept.*
1985): Bruce
Banner faces death
in a nightmarish
dimension. (Cover
by Mike Mignola
and Al Williamson)

1986

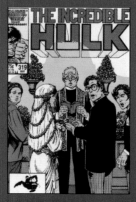

Hulk #319 *(May*
1986): Bruce
Banner finally
marries Betty Ross.
(Cover by John
Byrne)

1987

Hulk #336 *(Oct.*
1987): The Hulk
battles X-Factor.
(Cover by Steve
Geiger and Bob
McLeod)

THE U-FOES™

YEARS AGO, A SIMILAR FOURSOME GATHERED ON A NIGHT SUCH AS THIS! THEIR GOAL--TO FLY A SHIP TO THE MOON!

FANTASTIC FOUR

THEY NEVER REACHED THEIR DESTINATION! COSMIC RAYS PENETRATED THEIR SHIP-- THEIR VERY CELLS--TRANSFORMING THEM INTO THE FANTASTIC FOUR!

THE SMALLEST DETAIL
Simon was determined to copy everything about the Fantastic Four's original flight into space. He even tracked down the contractors who built the F.F.'s spaceship and bribed them to provide the necessary specifications.

SIMON UTRECHT was a former politician and self-made millionaire. He seemed to have everything a man could ask for, but he wanted more. Simon desired superhuman power. In an attempt to duplicate the accident that created the Fantastic Four, he financed the construction of a private spaceship. Needing three additional crewmen, he scoured the personal files of thousands of employees and interviewed a few hundred candidates. In due time, he choose Michael Steel as his pilot, along with Ann Darnell, a life-support engineer and her brother Jimmy Darnell, a fuel-propulsion expert.

Simon intended to expose his team to cosmic rays and gain super-powers that could be used to make him even richer and more famous. His plan might actually have worked, if it hadn't been for the Hulk…

X-Ray (Jimmy Darnell) is a being of pure energy who can fly and fire blasts of radiation at his enemies.

Ironclad (Mike Steel) possesses superhuman strength and can increase his weight at will.

No Good Deed Goes Unpunished

The Hulk wandered into the vicinity of Simon's fully automated command center on the night of the launch. After changing into Bruce Banner, he watched as the spaceship blasted off. The confused scientist entered Simon's deserted installation and was horrified when he observed the crew being bombarded by cosmic rays. Banner reprogrammed their flight computer and brought the ship back to Earth. Since he was only trying to save their lives, Banner was surprised when Simon's team attacked him.

Vapor (Ann Darnell) can convert her body into any type of gas.

Vector (Simon Utrecht) can telekinetically lift and hurl almost any object.

Waiting for the U-Foes!

Simon's plan worked. He and his crew had been physically transformed by their trip into space, but he was still furious with Banner. Believing that they could have absorbed even more power from the cosmic rays if Banner hadn't interfered, Simon ordered the team to kill him.

Unfamiliar with their new powers, the U-Foes kept getting in each other's way and gave the Hulk ample opportunity to defeat them.

STORM WARNINGS
Utrecht waited until his tracking satellites informed him that a cosmic storm, similar to the one that gave the F.F. their powers, was brewing above the Earth's atmosphere. Anxious to absorb as many cosmic rays as possible, he programmed his flight so that his ship would arrive just as the storm hit its peak.

The Day of Their Return
The U-Foes later reformed, practiced together, and learned how to control their powers. They ambushed Bruce Banner and took him prisoner. X-Ray discovered that he could use negative gamma rays to keep the Hulk in his human form. The team planned to kill the Hulk in front of a televised audience and position themselves as heroes.

POWER DRAIN
While Banner was their prisoner, the U-Foes bound him to an energy grid that rained a constant flow of negative gamma rays over him and prevented him from transforming into the Hulk.

FRIENDS TO THE RESCUE
With the help of Rick Jones and Betty Ross, Bereet used her robot-like toys to distract the U-Foes long enough for Banner to turn the tables on them.

ALMOST INVINCIBLE
Ironclad has never been able to accept that the Hulk is more powerful than he is. Mike Steel has challenged the green giant to numerous fights and has lost every one.

STILL AT LARGE
The government later offered the U-Foes an early release from prison if they agreed to relinquish their super-powers. They escaped during the procedure and tracked the Hulk to the Crossroads of Eternity. After returning to Earth, they attacked the Avengers and later formed an alliance with the Leader. They recently stormed the United Nations Plaza where some of the world's top scientists were meeting, but were eventually driven off by the Hulk.

Though he can increase his weight without growing in size, Ironclad usually tips the scales at 650 lb and stands 6 ft 7 in in his bare feet.

THE SOVIET SUPER-SOLDIERS ™

HAVING OBSERVED THE AMERICANS form teams of superhuman adventurers like the Fantastic Four and the Avengers, the former Soviet government commissioned Professor Piotr Phobos, a latent mutant himself, to locate and train potential super heroes. Hundreds of candidates were selected, but very few survived the rigorous program. Mikhail Uriokovitch Ursus (Ursa Major) was a mutant who could transform into a large bear-like creature. Nikolai Krylenko and Laynia Petrovna were twins born with mutant powers. Nikolai (Vanguard) could generate a force field that could repel any form of energy and Laynia (Darkstar) discovered that she could tap into and manipulate an extradimensional source of energy called the Darkforce. These Super-Soldiers were teamed with a super-agent named the Crimson Dynamo.

The Russian version of Iron Man, many agents have worn the armor of the Crimson Dynamo.

BETRAYED
Placed under the command of the Russian K.G.B., the team became the official super heroes of the former Soviet Union. They were sent to investigate a radioactive wasteland near Khystym where they encountered the Hulk. During the course of their battle, the Super-Soldiers learned that Professor Phobos had been secretly siphoning their powers to supplement his own.

TEAMING WITH TITANIUM MAN

After being assigned a few distasteful missions for the K.G.B., the Super-Soldiers threw the Crimson Dynamo off the team, severed their ties with the government and aided the people of their country without official sanction. They returned to Khystym where they met the Gremlin and learned that an alien race planned to invade Russia. After defeating the aliens, the Gremlin designed a new Titanium Man combat suit for himself and temporarily joined the team.

Transformation from man to beast takes ten seconds; Mikhail retains his human intelligence.

Forced into Exile

Though they continued to protect the Russian people from super-menaces, relations between the Super-Soldiers and their government continued to deteriorate. They were eventually declared traitors and forced to flee the country. The Super-Soldiers asked Captain America for political asylum and remained in the U.S. until the fall of the Soviet Union.

Ursa Major possesses superhuman strength in beast form, but the Hulk is far stronger.

Darkstar can use her Darkforce to fly and can also form solid objects out of it.

Vanguard wields a special hammer and sickle designed to focus and intensify his repelling force.

IT IS A MONSTER -- SNARLING THREATS IN ENGLISH!

SABRA

BORN NEAR THE CITY of Jerusalem, Ruth Bat-Seraph began to exhibit mutant like abilities while still a child. Her parents took her to a special kibbutz where the Israeli government studied her emerging powers and trained her how to use them. She was later enrolled in a government-sponsored "super-agent" program and given the code-name Sabra. Though secretly an agent for Mossad, the Israeli secret service, Ruth became a police officer to cover her superhuman activities. She first encountered the Hulk after he arrived in the cargo hold of a ship that had docked in Tel Aviv. Disoriented by his surroundings, Bruce Banner made the acquaintance of a young Arab who was later killed by terrorists. Sabra came upon the Hulk moments after he subdued the killers, but she mistakenly believed that he was one of them.

SUPER COP
When Sabra was offered her choice of undercover assignments, she decided to become a police officer. In contrast to her secret government missions, she gets a real sense of achievement from helping the public.

GOOD! IF THEY CAN WEAK-EN HIM, THEN PERHAPS AN *OVERDOSE* CAN BRING HIM DOWN!

GRAARH!

Lethal Lady
The official protector of Israel, Sabra possesses superhuman strength, speed, reflexes, endurance, and recuperative powers. Her skin, muscle and bone are denser than normal, giving her natural body armor. She is skilled in all forms of personal combat and has been trained in police methods and anti-terrorist techniques. Her main weapons are wrist bracelets that shoot energy quills of low-density plasma. These travel at the speed of sound and can paralyze a man for an hour or more.

LITTLE HITLER

Sabra later encountered the Hulk while he was working for the Pantheon. She was assigned to protect a 13-year-old mutant that the Hulk had learned was destined to lead his country into a war that would result in the deaths of millions. Sabra managed to fight the Hulk to a standstill, but the child was later trampled by a crowd that he had incited to riot.

Sabra's cape contains a device that neutralizes gravity and allows her to fly at over 300 mph.

ARABIAN KNIGHT

Nomadic Champion
Abdul Qamar, a Bedouin chieftain, found Bruce Banner unconscious in the Sahara desert and gave him shelter. A few days later, Abdul entered an ancient tomb and found a golden scimitar that could emit beams of concussive force, a belt-sash that could serve as a lariat, whip, or climbing rope, and a flying carpet that obeyed his will. With these magical weapons, Abdul battled evil as the Arabian Knight.

THIS CHAMBER--IT APPEARS TO WEATHER THE EARTHQUAKE MORE SOLIDLY THAN THE REST OF THE CRYPT! PERHAPS I SHALL BE *SAFE* HERE UNTIL THE WORKERS DIG ME OUT!

EH? THAT GLOWING SCIMITAR LYING ACROSS AN ORNATE RUG--!

IT SEEMS OF A DIFFERENT AGE ALTOGETHER FROM THE CRYPT! CAN THIS BE THE SACRED SCIMITAR OF WHICH OUR LEGENDS SPEAK?

FINAL TRAGEDY
Working with the Hulk, the Arabian Knight defeated a horde of demonic creatures that sought to conquer Egypt. Unfortunately, Abdul was later killed in a random accident.

THE CROSSROADS

AFTER THE HULK gained the intelligence and personality of Bruce Banner, a nightmarish creature from another dimension transformed him into a savage beast. He no longer possessed a human mind to temper his anger and went totally berserk. The Amazing Spider-Man, Daredevil, and the Avengers joined forces to subdue the bludgeoning behemoth. Since Earth was no longer safe from Hulk, Doctor Strange attempted to help his former teammate by finding a new home for him. The master of mysticism began to search the multiverse for an alternate reality where the Hulk could finally find happiness. Strange used his magic to exile the Hulk to a place where many different dimensions converged, a nexus of reality called The Crossroads of Eternity.

WORLDS UNTOLD
Many alternate worlds existed where the Hulk could have raged to his heart's content, but Doctor Strange was morally bound to choose one where old Greenskin couldn't harm or be harmed by the inhabitants. The master mystic cast a spell that returned the Hulk to the Crossroads whenever a new world proved unsuitable for him.

The Games Aliens Play

After briefly exploring the Crossroads, the Hulk chose a path that led him to a world that appeared to be at war. He had army tanks, jet fighters, and a city to smash, but soon realized that something was wrong. The city wasn't real: it was part of a sophisticated play set that belonged to a giant alien child. The Hulk had no interest in playing games. He instinctively triggered Strange's fail-safe spell and returned to the Crossroads to choose another world.

KILLED BY COMPASSION

Since there was no food at the Crossroads, the Hulk journeyed to a world covered with purple vegetation, where he soon discovered a creature as powerful as himself. The alien befriended the green Goliath and showed him which plants were safe to eat and where to find shelter. Imprisoned on this world by his warlike race, the alien was eventually sentenced to death for showing forbidden emotions.

CITY OF DEATH
Drawn to a medieval world by a green-skinned maiden who reminded him of Jarella, the Hulk was shocked to discover a city of death that had been constructed of skulls and bones. He also learned that this world was ruled by a race of Iron Knights that possessed super-strength far greater than his own. Enslaved and used as a beast of burden by the Knights, the Hulk didn't trigger his fail-safe spell until after he helped the maiden lead a revolution to free her world.

Banner's Return
In a barbarian world, the Hulk was struck by a poisoned spear. It caused his body to grow weak and turned him back into Bruce Banner for nearly a year. Banner used his time at the Crossroads to resolve some of his feelings toward his father. He eventually returned to Earth, thanks to the efforts of Dr. Walter Langkowski.

Seeking to exploit the Hulk's power for their own dark desires, various demonic creatures sought to lure him into their own devilish worlds.

KLAATU THE CURSED
Before leaving the Crossroads, the crew of the starship Andromeda forced the Hulk to join the hunt for a 500-foot-tall space-spawned leviathan called Klaatu. But the Hulk identified with this raging monster and freed it after energy-leeching harpoons ensnared it.

The Triad
The Triad are subconscious projections that helped the Hulk regain his psychic connection to Bruce Banner. Glow was a star that hung above Banner's crib and represented reason. Guardian was a gift from his mother and its arrows filled the Hulk with awareness. Goblin symbolized Bruce's rage and reminded him of his father.

PUFFBALL COLLECTIVE

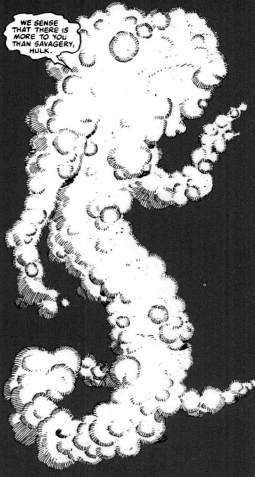

WE SENSE THAT THERE IS MORE TO YOU THAN SAVAGERY, HULK.

Sinister Spheres
Originally from a world where they floated free, the Puffball Collective is composed of thousands of tiny balls of consciousness united to form a single entity. It can read minds and mimic any shape it desires. The balls can also separate and assume multiple forms. The Collective pretended to be the Hulk's friend so that it could use his power to return to its homeworld.

BUT YOU, HULK, HAVE RENDERED THEIR SACRIFICE SENSELESS!

THANKS TO YOUR SAVAGE STRENGTH, THE PORTAL IS UNSEALED!

UNDER OUR COMMAND, THE DEMONS SHALL NOW SALLY FORTH-- UNSTOPPABLE-- TO TAKE OVER OTHER WORLDS!

BUT FIRST, OF COURSE, THEY MUST DEAL WITH ... YOU!

BANISHED BALLS
Malignant balls dabbled with mystic forces and released demons on their world. The other puffballs banished the evil Collective to the Crossroads.

SEPARATED HULK™

BELIEVING THAT BRUCE BANNER was actually a prisoner trapped within the Hulk, Doc Samson persuaded the U.S. government to fund a radical procedure to save the scientist. Heading *Operation: Rescue*, Samson captured the Hulk and attempted to identify all the organic matter that was uniquely Banner and edit it out of the green giant's body. The trickiest part was making sure Banner's intellect went into the new body, leaving the Hulk's mind a blank slate devoid of any memories. As a psychologist, Samson was excited by the prospect of reeducating and training the new Hulk, convinced that the creature could someday enter society as a fully functioning human. However, Doc Samson soon learned that the government had lied to him and planned to kill the new Hulk.

The Calm and the Storm

After being removed from Samson's nutrient bath, Bruce Banner lay in a coma until an experimental psychic-stimulation formula shocked him awake. He remained in a weakened condition for several weeks, but gradually recovered. Convinced he was now cured, Bruce asked Betty Ross to marry him. Meanwhile, no longer restrained by Banner's influence, the Hulk became a creature of mindless, undiluted rage.

Having grown to nearly twice his usual size, the Hulk was becoming progressively weaker until the Vision found a way to reconnect him with Bruce Banner.

DEATH MATCH
While the Avengers tried to subdue the mindless Hulk, Bruce Banner collapsed on his honeymoon. His body started to expand, growing so large that it began to lose its structure. The same began to happen to the Hulk. Doc Samson realized they would both die unless reunited.

CERTAIN INTANGIBLES

Unable to reason with or to stop the brainless beast that the Hulk had become, the Avengers knew their only recourse was to destroy him. Their strongest members united in a single attack that stunned and toppled the creature. As they prepared to deliver the deathblow, Betty Banner burst on the scene and begged for the life of her husband. Realizing that the life of an innocent man was at stake, the heroes took pity on her. An android called the Vision had the ability to control his density. He somehow managed to draw Banner's molecules back together and reintegrate them with those of the Hulk.

RICK JONES-HULK™

While attempting to destroy the original Hulk, General Ross accidentally created a new one!

EVEN THOUGH the Vision enabled Banner and the Hulk to mesh again, their union proved unstable. Doc Samson realized that their only hope was to reverse the process that originally separated them and put them back in the nutrient bath. While Samson made the necessary preparations, Rick Jones discovered that General Ross intended to sabotage the procedure and kill Banner and the Hulk. Rick tried to stop the General, but was hurled into the bath. His presence altered the chemical reaction and caused an explosion. The Hulk emerged from the wreckage, his skin gray instead of green. Rick Jones was also changed. He was now cursed to transform into a Hulk-like creature.

The Rick Jones Hulk-like creature was almost as powerful as the Hulk, but did not grow stronger as he got angrier.

THERE CAN ONLY BE ONE
Though unable to help himself, Bruce Banner believed that it was still possible to cure Rick and gambled his own life to save his friend.

DANCE WITH THE DEVIL

A new greenskinned monster haunted the countryside for the next few weeks. The authorities suspected Banner at first, until the new Hulk attacked him. Realizing that time was running out for Rick, the scientist turned to his old enemy the Leader for help and deliberately transformed himself into the grayskinned Hulk. After battling the Rick version into submission, Banner saved his friend by draining the gamma radiation from his body and sending it into the Leader.

Monster Hunt

While Bruce Banner was temporarily separated from the Hulk, the U.S. government commissioned him to assemble an elite paramilitary team called the Hulkbusters to track down and capture the escaped monster. Banner chose five core members: Craig Saunders, a demolition specialist; Carolyn Parmenter, a marine biologist; Samuel J. LaRoquette, an explorer and authority on survival techniques; Dr. Armand Martel, a xeno-biologist; and Professor Hideko Takata, a geophysicist. Although they were experts in their fields, they all had tragic pasts and were in desperate need of a second chance.

LEGACY OF FAILURE
The Hulkbusters were armed with sophisticated combat vehicles, but did not cover themselves in glory. Carolyn Parmenter died during a training exercise. To make matters worse, the Hulk defeated the Hulkbusters every time he fought them. Martel and Takata quit the team in disgust. Determined to complete the mission, LaRoquette and Saunders joined the Leader.

ROCK™ AND REDEEMER™

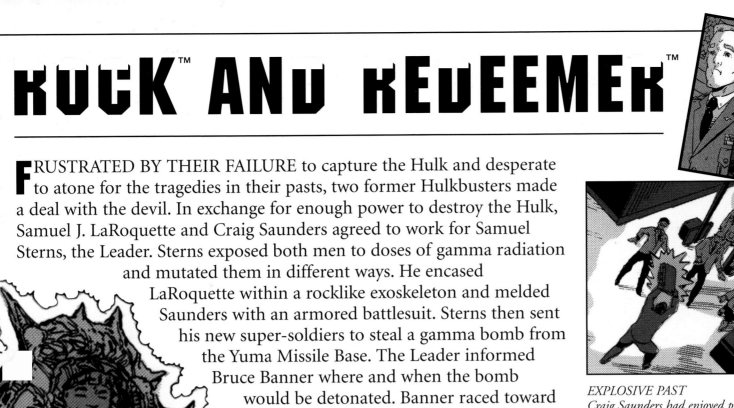

FRUSTRATED BY THEIR FAILURE to capture the Hulk and desperate to atone for the tragedies in their pasts, two former Hulkbusters made a deal with the devil. In exchange for enough power to destroy the Hulk, Samuel J. LaRoquette and Craig Saunders agreed to work for Samuel Sterns, the Leader. Sterns exposed both men to doses of gamma radiation and mutated them in different ways. He encased LaRoquette within a rocklike exoskeleton and melded Saunders with an armored battlesuit. Sterns then sent his new super-soldiers to steal a gamma bomb from the Yuma Missile Base. The Leader informed Bruce Banner where and when the bomb would be detonated. Banner raced toward a small city called Middletown, where he had a date with Rock and Redeemer.

EXPLOSIVE PAST
Craig Saunders had enjoyed playing with caps and blowing things up ever since he was a child. He joined the military and became a demolitions expert. However, his life fell apart when he failed to defuse a bomb in a crowded airport terminal and two civilians died.

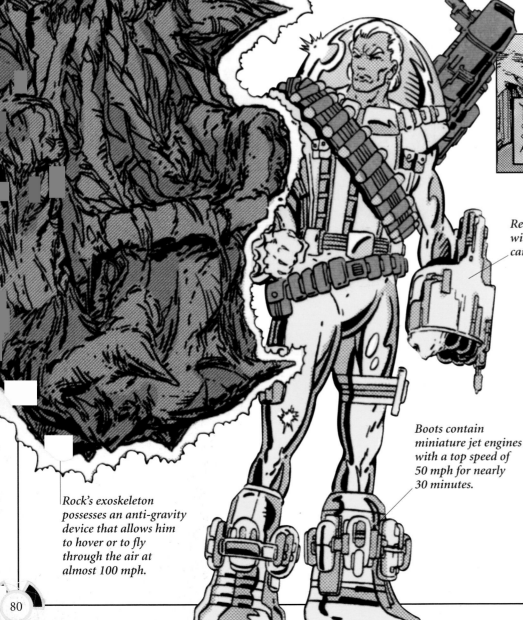

Your last expedition resulted in the hideous deaths of two of your people when an earthquake struck. The very planet had turned against you.

A HARD MAN
LaRoquette's favorite childhood toy was an old refrigerator with the door off. He used to pretend it was a submarine or spaceship. He grew up to live out some of those fantasies, but his temper often got him into trouble with his superiors. Believing everyone was against him, LaRoquette built a tough shell around himself.

Redeemer is armed with twin plasma canons on both hands.

Boots contain miniature jet engines with a top speed of 50 mph for nearly 30 minutes.

Rock's exoskeleton possesses an anti-gravity device that allows him to hover or to fly through the air at almost 100 mph.

GROUND ZERO

After trying to evacuate the town, the Hulk began to search for the gamma bomb and that's when Rock and Redeemer attacked him. Redeemer blasted him in the face with enough concussive force to shatter an army tank, but the Hulk merely shrugged it off. After forming a massive foot, Rock tried to kick old Greenskin into orbit. The Hulk hurled him away and crushed Redeemer's hand cannons. The Leader appeared and distracted the Hulk long enough for Rock to stab him in the back. The Hulk found the bomb, but was unable to stop it from exploding and obliterating Middletown.

FULLY LOADED
Redeemer was bio-engineered so that his body was permanently connected to his mobile combat suit. The armor was constructed from an experimental alloy that was much lighter and tougher than any commercially available material. It came equipped with a rocket and grenade launcher and various other offensive weapons.

Back from the Dead
Craig Saunders was killed during his first battle with the Hulk when he was sent crashing into Rock's spike-like exterior. LaRoquette blamed himself, just like he did when Hulkbuster Carolyn Parmenter perished, and he wanted revenge. The Leader was only too happy to help him achieve it. After capturing and brainwashing General Ross, the Leader temporarily put the Hulk's father-in-law into Redeemer's old battlesuit.

Supple Stone
Composed of an unknown substance invented by the Leader, Rock's exoskeleton can be molded into any shape he desires. He can also extend his spikes while spinning at great speed. Rock feels intense physical pain whenever his exoskeleton is damaged.

BROKEN DREAMS
Rock and the new Redeemer joined forces with the U-Foes and Riot Squad and invaded the Pantheon's mountain headquarters in search of the Hulk. The Leader arranged a truce with the Pantheon's leader, and when Hydra attacked Freehold (the Leader's self-proclaimed Utopia), Rock found himself teamed with the Hulk. Realizing that he would never be able to conquer the Hulk, Rock retired to Freehold, where he remains today.

HALFLIFE

Like a Vampire
Tony Masterson was a schoolteacher until he was accidentally exposed to gamma rays. The radiation appeared to kill Tony, but he arose every night hungry for the energy he could only drain from living bodies. Halflife set his sights on the Hulk, hoping to absorb enough energy from him to remain alive during the day. When the Hulk convinced Halflife that he would never regain his humanity, the creature lost the will to live and withered away.

Halflife could detach his limbs and reassemble himself. He absorbed his victim's life force by wrapping himself around them.

JOE FIXIT ™

H E WAS THE MYSTERY MAN of Las Vegas, a massive figure that kept to the shadows. His name was Joe Fixit and he worked at the Coliseum. His title was "Director of Special Occasions," but everyone knew that he was an enforcer who reported directly to the casino's owner, Michael Berengetti. Joe Fixit lived in the hotel's best suite, enjoyed gourmet meals, dated beautiful women, and wore expensive clothes, and all he had to do was occasionally beat up people. Joe's skin had a grayish hue but no one ever guessed the truth. Joe Fixit was secretly the incredible Hulk. Mere moments before the Leader detonated the gamma bomb that eradicated Middletown, the Hulk had been magically transported back to Jarella's world. A zealot who had built a religion around the Hulk was now menacing the former paradise. After toppling the would-be dictator, the Hulk obtained a magic spell that could prevent him from transforming back into Bruce Banner and he returned to Earth.

BEHEMOTH BODYGUARD

Michael Berengetti found the Hulk dazed and wandering the desert near Yucca Flats. The spell that had returned him from Jarella's world had gone awry and left the gray-skinned Goliath looking like he had been through a cement mixture. After naming him Joe after Mighty Joe Young, his favorite big gorilla, Berengetti brought the Hulk to the Coliseum and offered him a job as a leg-breaker.

Tired of being dressed in Banner's rags, Joe Fixit wore tailor-made suits and enjoyed a life of conspicuous consumption.

MUSCLED BY THE MAGGIA
Not long after Joe Fixit began working at the Coliseum, an international crime syndicate called the Maggia tried to seize control of the casino. They threatened Berengetti and even blew up his house, but they were eventually driven off by the power of the Hulk.

A Class Act

Michael Berengetti epitomized style and subtlety. A man of honor who never broke his word, he was the only one who ever gave the Hulk a good life and didn't betray him. Michael truly liked the Hulk, but had to fire him when his growing temper tantrums began to frighten the casino owner. When a business rival later murdered Berengetti, the Hulk returned to Las Vegas to avenge his former boss.

HAUNTED BY BANNER
After months of being free from Banner, the Hulk began to feel the scientist clawing at the back of his mind, desperate to break free. The Hulk started to grow weak during the day and direct sunlight hurt him, as if it was trying to burn him away. Realizing that the spell from Jarella's world was wearing off, the Hulk resorted to meditation to keep Banner locked inside, but even that failed.

AND WHAT THE BULLETS STARTED...

...I'LL FINISH!

Since the world believed he had died when Middletown exploded, the Hulk created a new identity for himself.

A SEPARATE PEACE
When Banner awoke in Joe Fixit's bed, he had no idea where he was or how much time had passed. He was dismayed to discover that the Hulk had landed him in the middle of a power struggle between Michael Berengetti and the Maggia. Pretending to be Joe Fixit's half-brother, Banner communicated with the Hulk by a series of notes and they began to gain a better understanding of each other. In the past, Banner had always hated the Hulk, but now he started to sympathize with him. For the first time, Banner and the Hulk worked together, forging a truce that lasted many months.

WELL, HULK...

WHATEVER YOU'RE INVOLVED WITH, YOU JUST LET ME KNOW HOW *IMPORTANT* IT IS TO YOU.

THAT WAS YOUR *FIRST* MISTAKE.

HULK V. IRON MAN
Angry about what happened in Las Vegas, the Hulk faked a war with Iron Man as part of a scheme to bilk the Maggia out of a million dollars.

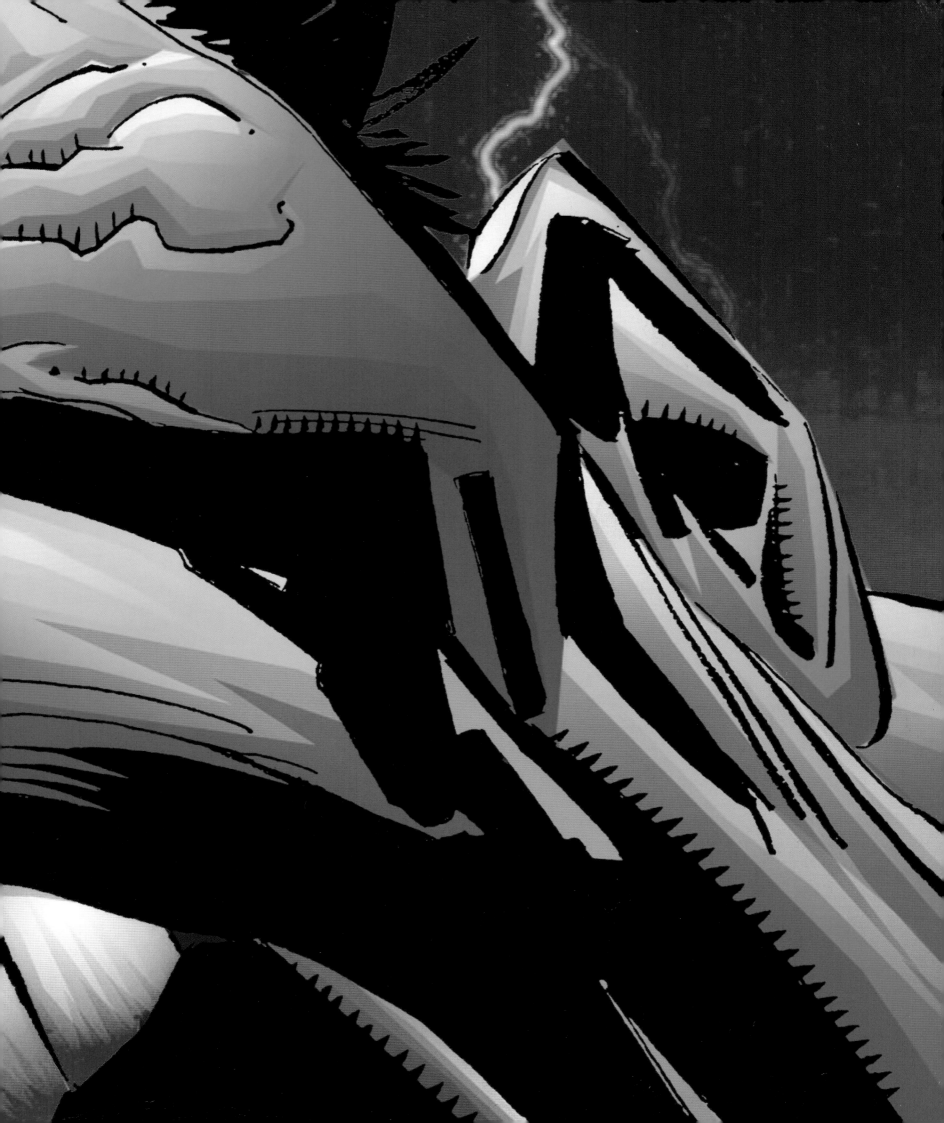

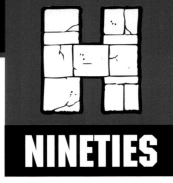
THE DECADE BEGAN on a haunting note with the airing of *The Death of the Incredible Hulk*, the final television movie to star Bill Bixby and Lou Ferrigno. Though a sequel tentatively entitled *The Resurrection of the Incredible Hulk* was planned, it never materialized.

Coincidentally, the Hulk had been injected with a deadly toxin and was also dying in the comic books. He recovered as artist Jeff Purves ended his run and Dale Keown joined writer Peter David. Over the next few months, the original Defenders reunited and Bruce revived his marriage with Betty. Doc Samson found a way to integrate the crafty gray Hulk with the savage green one to form an amalgam that came to be known as the Professor. Possessing Banner's intelligence with the Hulk's appearance, this new Hulk joined an organization called the Pantheon and prevented the kind of disasters he used to incite. Rick Jones started dating Joe Fixit's former girlfriend Marlo and married her. Jan Duursema briefly took over the art chores as the Hulk faced a ghost from the past and made his first trip to Freehold, the Leader's paradise. Penciler Gary Frank illustrated a series of stories that featured return bouts with the Juggernaut and the Avengers. The Hulk journeyed into deep space to fight in the Troyjan War and visited Asgard, home of the Norse gods.

Hulk #413 *(Jan. 1994): The Hulk leads the Pantheon into outer space. (Cover by Gary Frank and Cam Smith)*

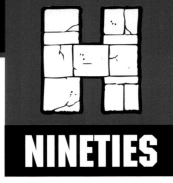

Following the fall of the Pantheon, Peter David was teamed with a succession of artists that included Derrick Robertson, Liam Sharpe, Terry Dodson, Angel Medina, Mike Deodato, Jr., George Perez and Adam Kubert as the Hulk turned into the Savage Banner whenever he got angry and soon became radioactive. He journeyed to an alternate future where he met the granddaughter of Rick Jones and an evil incarnation of himself called the Maestro. As Peter David prepared to leave the book, he stunned Hulk fans with the tragic death of Betty Ross.

After publishing *Incredible Hulk* for over three decades, Marvel Comics decided to relaunch the Hulk's comic book and hired writer Joe Casey and artist Javier Pulido to wrap up the current series. Called simply *Hulk* (although *The Incredible* was later added), the greenskinned Goliath prepared to enter the new millennium with a new title under the guidance of writer John Byrne and artist Ron Garney.

Future Imperfect (1993): The graphic novel that introduces the Maestro, the Hulk's future self. (Cover by George Perez)

1990

Hulk #371 *(July 1990): The original Defenders reunite as Banner loses control of the Hulk. (Cover by Dale Keown)*

1992

Hulk #393 *(May 1992): 30 years of the Hulk are celebrated. (Cover by Dale Keown after Jack Kirby)*

1994

Hulk #420 *(Aug. 1994): The death of Jim Wilson. (Cover by Gary Frank and Cam Smith)*

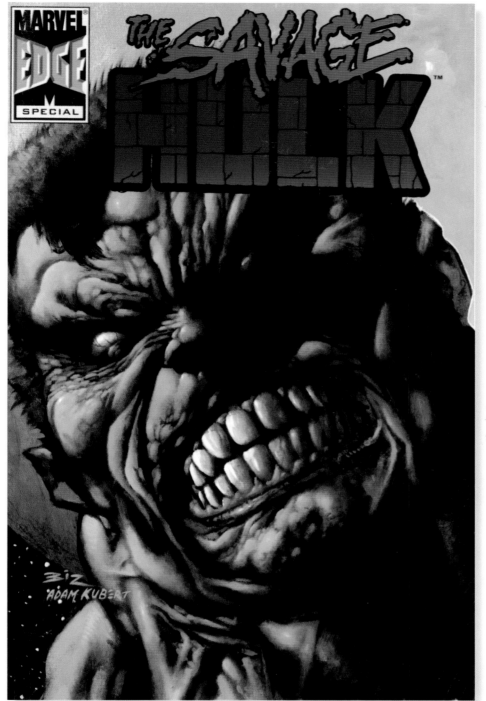

Hulk Magazine #1 *(Dec. 1996):*
A regular, 100-page magazine
devoted to everyone's favorite engine of
destruction. (Cover by Adam Kubert
and Mark Farmer)

The Savage Hulk *(Jan. 1996): The*
Hulk confronts his past. (Painting by
Simon Bisley and Adam Kubert)

1996

Hulk-Hercules
Unleashed *(Oct.*
1996): A special
one-shot featuring
the hero of Greek
myth. (Cover by
Mike Deodato, Jr.)

1998

The Rampaging
Hulk #1 *(Aug.*
1998): A new title
that featured untold
tales of the Hulk's
past. (Cover by Rick
Leonardi)

1999

Hulk #1 *(April*
1999): Though no
longer incredible,
the Hulk's title is
relaunched for the
new millennium.
(Cover by Ron
Garney)

THE PANTHEON

THEY ONLY WANT TO save the world. The Pantheon is a worldwide organization founded by an immortal named Agamemnon. Claiming that his mother was an Earth woman and his father a god, Aggy observed humanity for centuries. He also assumed dozens of identities and fathered hundreds of children. Agamemnon dreamed of improving the human condition and bringing an end to war, famine, and pestilence. He assembled a massive think tank to accomplish his dream. Super-teams like the Avengers and the Defenders only reacted to emergencies after they occurred; Aggy formed the Pantheon to spot potential disasters and prevent them. His communications center was patched into every news organization and he placed agents in most major governments.

AMAZING ACCOMPLISHMENTS

The Pantheon employed thousands of scientists, doctors and technicians, who advanced existing branches of knowledge and created new ones. Their medical researchers developed more efficient skin graft techniques to help burn victims and were still attempting to find cures for heart disease, cancer and AIDS. The Pantheon took in children who had been orphaned by war and found homes for them. They also supplied food and farming equipment to starving nations.

PEOPLE NOT POLITICS
The Pantheon's belief in human rights often led it to side with rebels against tyranny. Although it tried to avoid needless violence, it would gear up for war if the cause seemed just. The Pantheon's efforts brought it into direct conflict with the United Nations and the US government.

The Pantheon had access to super-weapons that were light years ahead of conventional armaments.

THIS HULK FOR HIRE
After Doc Samson helped Bruce merge his multiple personalities into the Professor, Agamemnon asked the Hulk to join the Pantheon. The Hulk was reluctant at first. He changed his mind because he saw an opportunity to atone for past acts of destruction and to help the world. While with the Pantheon, the Hulk prevented a would-be dictator from starting a world war, traveled into space and journeyed to Asgard, home of the Norse gods.

Possessing the intelligence of Bruce Banner, the Hulk no longer dressed in tattered shirts and torn purple trousers, but he did like his bunny slippers.

ADLANNA! YOOR OKAY!

I SAFED YOO!

SURE I'M OKAY, BIG GUY. I'M PRETTY STURDY, AND BESIDES, I GOT *YOU* AROUND TO WATCH MY BACK, HEY?

Touched by Godhood

The core members of the Pantheon were all part of Agamemnon's extended family. They lived exceptionally long lives and many of them possessed superhuman abilities. Achilles was invulnerable to pretty much everything, except when the Hulk was around. For some reason, any source of gamma radiation made Achilles susceptible to harm. Atalanta was a woman warrior who fired arrows of pure energy. Ajax was a simple-minded giant who possessed superhuman strength, but needed a special environment suit to support his massive weight.

CHILDISH BEHAVIOR
Despite their powers, the Pantheon members often acted like spoiled children. They squabbled and played pranks on each other. Paris hated his brother Ulysses and delighted in undermining his authority. Ajax worshiped Atalanta, but she dated Achilles behind his back. The Hulk had to step in when Ajax found out and almost killed his distant cousin.

The Pantheon employed a heavily armed vehicle that could travel on land, under the water, or in the air.

THE MOUNT
The Pantheon's base was located on a plateau somewhere in northern Arizona. It contained every facility required to house a population of nearly 1,500 people. The Mount included laboratories, a hospital, and a hydroponics farm that supplied most of the food. A weapons factory, motor pool, plane hangar, and heliport rounded out the accommodations.

The Endless Knights

When the Pantheon learned that Agamemnon had betrayed them, they put him on trial for his life. He laughed at their arrogance and summoned the Endless Knights, an unstoppable army of zombie warriors that consisted of deceased members of the Pantheon. After evacuating all the civilians from the Mount, the Hulk led the remaining Pantheon in their final battle.

Agamemnon

A holographic image portrayed him as an old man, but he really looked like a teenager. Agamemnon was immortal, but his offspring were not. In exchange for the technology to augment their life spans, Agamemnon offered an alien race called the Troyjans their pick of his descendants.

MADMAN™

Phil suffered from a split personality and often had long talks with his reflection in mirrors.

EVEN SUPER-VILLAINS have families, and that includes Samuel Sterns, the Leader. Sam had a younger brother named Phil. Though the smarter of the Sterns boys, Phil barely managed to squeak through college. He wanted to become a nuclear physicist and attended the same graduate school as Bruce Banner. Phil admired Banner's brilliance, but always from afar. Banner was top of the class while Phil hovered near the bottom. After graduation, Phil eked out a living and kept track of Banner's career. When he found out that Banner had become the Hulk, he decided to follow in his hero's footsteps and exposed himself to gamma radiation. Phil was transformed into a grotesque creature called Madman. Madman was far smarter and more aggressive than Phil, who soon found himself dominated by his alter ego.

Countdown
While working at the Yucca Flats Nuclear Research Laboratory, Phil recognized Banner who was masquerading as a janitor to avoid the authorities. Always jealous of Banner, Madman ordered Phil to inject him with a slow-acting poison. The Hulk began to waste away and was only seconds away from death when he finally obtained the antidote.

Madman is able to shift his shape to resemble anyone he chooses.

BULKING UP
Phil and Madman have very different personalities. Phil is quiet and shy and Madman boisterous and confident. Madman can expand his size at will. He can grow from his normal height of 5 ft 10 in to 10 ft in moments, and increase his weight from 140 lb to nearly 2,000 lb. Although he can only remain this way for a few seconds, he is nearly twice as strong as the Hulk while at maximum size.

MADMAN! PUT HIM DOWN SLOWLY AND BACK AWAY!

WHAT'S YOUR PROBLEM, BANNER!? THIS IS WHAT IT'S ALL ABOUT!

Madman has the stamina and durability of the Hulk.

ROYAL PAIN

After helping the creature known as Piecemeal battle the Hulk, Madman decided that he was tired of being a super-villain. He wanted to retire to a nice quiet place where he could be surrounded by hordes of flunkies. He traveled to England, stormed the royal palace and took the Prince of Wales hostage. Madman threatened to kill the Prince unless he was given control of the country. The Hulk rescued the Prince and hurled Madman into the Thames, but his body was never recovered.

THE RIoT SQUAD™

OGRESS
Diane Shadley was a lawyer who often represented people she knew to be guilty. But as the Ogress, she was unable to speak and could only express herself with her fists.

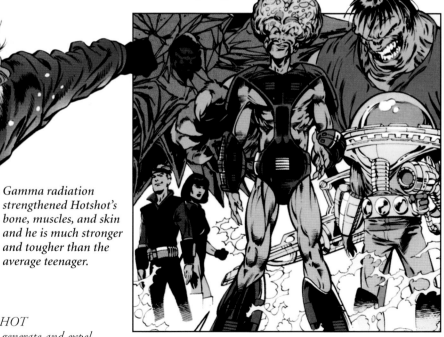

MIDDLETOWN WAS DYING. With a population under 5,000, it was an isolated little town surrounded by desert. The local textile factory had closed and many people were unemployed. It was the kind of town that no one would miss, which is probably why the Hulk's old enemy the Leader decided to expose it to gamma radiation. He hoped that some of its inhabitants would survive and join him in his new kingdom of Freehold. He sent Rock and Redeemer to steal a gamma bomb and planted it in Middletown. Only five people survived the blast: Father Jason McCall, a minister who had embezzled parish funds; Burt Horowitz, an encyclopedia salesman; Diane Shadley, a lawyer disgusted with her town, her practice and herself; Jessie Harrison, an impetuous 17-year-old; and Lou Stewart, her hotheaded boyfriend.

JAILBAIT
Jessie acquired the power to project beams of psionic energy from her mind and form them into cage-like constructs. These strong "energy cages" can imprison her enemies. Jailbait suffers a painful psychic backlash if they are ever shattered.

More beast than woman, the Ogress is almost as strong as the Hulk.

Hotshot can only produce a dozen energy balls before he becomes fatigued.

Come to Freehold!

When Diane, Jessie and Lou gained aggressive superhuman powers from their exposure to gamma rays, the Leader made them his personal bodyguards. Father McCall obtained the ability to reanimate corpses and began to call himself Soul Man. Horowitz became a human encyclopedia and took on the name of Omnibus. With Omnibus to advise him and the Riot Squad to protect him, the Leader used Soul Man to attract colonists to Freehold.

Gamma radiation strengthened Hotshot's bone, muscles, and skin and he is much stronger and tougher than the average teenager.

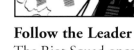

HOTSHOT
Lou can generate and expel balls of pure force from his hands. Each energy ball explodes on contact with the concussive force of a hand grenade. Lou never misses because he remains in mental contact with the balls and directs their various trajectories.

Follow the Leader
The Riot Squad once captured the Hulk and beat him unconscious. They also joined with Rock and Redeemer to invade the Pantheon's mountain headquarters. When Hydra attacked Freehold, the Leader appeared to die. The Riot Squad supported Omnibus's bid to lead Freehold until they learned that he was leading a worldwide criminal alliance.

MERCY

MERCY IS A strange visitor from a distant planet. A creature composed of pure psychic energy, she wandered the spaceways for thousands of years and visited countless worlds. She found herself drawn to Earth and was surprised to find a planet that contained so many unhappy people. Mercy decided to stay on this world and to make it a better place. She tried to improve the quality of life on Earth by eliminating everyone who was sad. Mercy appears to people who are overwhelmed by their problems and kills them as quickly and painlessly as possible. She doesn't think she's doing anything wrong. Mercy believes that she's on a holy mission. She's helping those who lack the strength to move away from this life and on to the next.

HELLO, ALFRED MY NEWEST LOVE!

WH-- WHAT'S ALL THIS?! CAN'T A BLOKE HAVE ANY PRIVACY? WHERE DID--

LIKE AN ANGEL
Mercy has no physical body. She has merely adapted her energy so that it looks human. She can travel through solid objects and transport herself to any destination with a single thought. Mercy is drawn to sad and lonely people. She can appear within a person's mind or disguise herself to look like anyone she chooses.

Mercy can float in the air or fly faster than a jet plane.

She can extend her hair to any length she desires and she can make each strand as tough as steel or as insubstantial as a dream.

HELLO, MY LOVE! FINALLY, WE'RE AWAY FROM ANY INNOCENT FOLKS.

YOU!

REJECTED
Mercy sensed the terrible burden that Bruce Banner was carrying and came to relieve his suffering. She was surprised to discover that two distinct beings were sharing the same existence and would never be happy until they were separated. Unable to grant their wish, Mercy tried to take away their pain by killing them, but neither one was ready to die. The Hulk and Banner both rejected her help by joining forces and driving Mercy away.

THE ENDLESS PAIN

Mercy couldn't believe that someone as angry and lonely as the Hulk could cling to life with such determination. After accidentally injuring Rick Jones, the Hulk became depressed and Mercy believed he was finally ready to die. She enlisted the aid of the Abomination to destroy him. That's when Mercy realized that the Hulk would never surrender to death. No matter how much pain or abuse he suffered, the Hulk would never stop fighting because he had to prove that he was the strongest one of all.

HULLO, WHO ARE YOU?

I'M ELIZABETH ROSS BANNER.

MY DADDY CALLS ME BETTY.

Betty's Choice

Betty Banner was seriously injured when the Endless Knights attacked the Pantheon. Sensing her connection to the Hulk, Mercy entered her mind and offered to end her suffering. Betty saw herself as a little child and wanted to be reunited with her deceased mother, but she couldn't desert Bruce. She knew how much he needed her and was willing to endure any misery to be with the man she loved. Betty refused Mercy's aid because she loved Bruce more than she loved herself.

SPEEDFЯEAK ™

LEON SHAPPE WAS A LOWLIFE, the type of petty criminal that real professionals avoided like the plague. No one trusted Leon. He had a big mouth and was addicted to a street drug called snap. The drug made him jittery and unreliable, and he would betray his own mother for a hit. Leon scraped a living stealing purses and robbing the elderly. He supplemented his income by working as a snitch for the police. One of his running buddies told him about an inventor who had built a mobile combat suit that could transform anyone into a one-man army. Leon murdered the inventor and stole the suit. His first instinct was to sell the suit, but he soon realized he could make more money by using it himself. For the first time in his life, Leon planned for the future. He became a professional assassin and called himself Speedfreak.

I WANT TO HAVE YOUR HUSBAND FIND AND BRING TO JUSTICE WHOEVER *KILLED* MY DAUGHTER.

Revenge
Leon loved his only daughter almost as much as he craved drugs. When he learned she had been killed, Leon disguised himself and hired the Hulk to find the person responsible. Unaware he was working for Speedfreak, the Hulk led him to the girl's ex-boyfriend who claimed her death was an accident. After nearly being disemboweled, the Hulk prevented Speedfreak from getting his revenge and turned the boy over to the authorities.

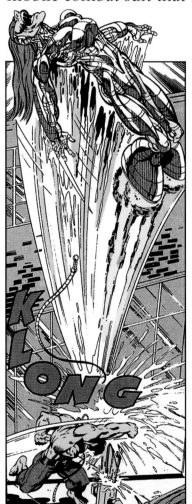

His arm sheaths contain adamantium swords that are sharp enough to decapitate the Hulk.

QUICK AND DEADLY
Speedfreak wears an armored exoskeleton composed of an experimental titanium steel alloy that is practically indestructible. It can resist small-arms fire and even the Hulk hasn't been able to dent it. His boots contain tractor threads that can propel him along at nearly 150 mph, and they also have built-in turbo-thrusters that allow him to fly.

Speedfreak's helmet has a transparent Plexiglas plate that lowers over his face when he's in flight and provides him with oxygen.

THE FAST AND THE FURIOUS

Even with his new powers, Leon's drug habit made him unreliable and he rarely received any important assignments. Speedfreak first met the Hulk at a charity event. A gang leader hired the assassin to kill a young man who was under the protection of Jim Wilson and Rick Jones. Speedfreak harpooned the Hulk with an adamantium-tipped barbed coil. The Hulk finally gained enough traction to break free and punch the would-be killer into the next township.

MAESTRO™

A SERIES OF nuclear wars devastated the Earth in one possible future. Radiation spread across the globe, killing the vast majority of the planet's inhabitants. One being benefited from all the destruction. Calling himself the Maestro, he soaked up radiation, becoming more powerful than ever before. He built the city of Dystopia and surrounded it with underground radiation-shielding generators. The Maestro ruled with an iron fist and tortured or murdered anyone who displeased him. A rebel band led by an ancient Rick Jones used a time machine to enlist the aid of the only man who had any hope of defeating the Maestro…

IT TAKES A HULK

When the present-day Rick Jones vouched for the rebels, the Hulk entered the time machine and journeyed across the years to fight the Maestro, *his own* future incarnation! The Hulk was shocked when he met the elderly version of Rick, who lived in a bunker surrounded by relics of all the super heroes that had died during the nuclear wars. Disgusted to hear of the Maestro's atrocities, the Hulk vowed to stop his future self.

GRAVITY POLICE
The Gravity Police were the Maestro's eyes and ears. They patrolled Dystopia in "float boats" that soared high above the streets. Encased in armored exoskeletons and armed with plasma blasters, they located any dissidents with citywide tracking systems.

STAY WHERE YOU ARE!

YOU HAVE BEEN IDENTIFIED AS INSURGENTS JANIS, PIZFIZ, SKOOTER AND DAKORD.

WE HAVE DISPATCHED DAKORD AS A *WARNING* TO THE REST OF YOU TO SURRENDER IMMEDIATELY.

ANY OR *ALL* OF YOU CAN BE DISPATCHED AS EASILY.

The Dogs ran at high speeds and leaped great distances.

THE DOGS O'WAR
The Maestro created the Dogs O'War to aid the Gravity Police. These creatures were part animal, part robot and completely vicious. Controlled by a human handler, who was physically melded to his mount, the dogs consumed anyone who dared to disturb the peace. Their bodies were fully armored, their teeth and claws razor-sharp and their jaws could crush adamantium steel, the strongest metal on Earth.

Though he possessed the genius of Bruce Banner, the Maestro had been driven mad by the same radiation that increased his strength.

CLASH OF THE HULKS

With his greater experience, the Maestro knew exactly how the Hulk thought and could anticipate his every move. The Maestro used his superior strength to break the Hulk's neck during their first battle. Knowing that he would soon heal, the Maestro took the Hulk prisoner and tried to win his loyalty by supplying him with beautiful companions and the best food. He built the paralyzed Hulk a floating chair and proudly gave him a tour of his kingdom. He explained his plans to reintroduce nutrients into the soil and his efforts to repopulate the Earth.

Thanks to additional radiation absorbed over the years, the Maestro was nearly twice as strong as the Hulk.

TO THE BEGINNING

The Maestro failed to corrupt the Hulk. Knowing he couldn't beat his future self in physical combat, the Hulk used the time machine to send the Maestro into the past. The same gamma bomb that originally created the Hulk incinerated the Maestro.

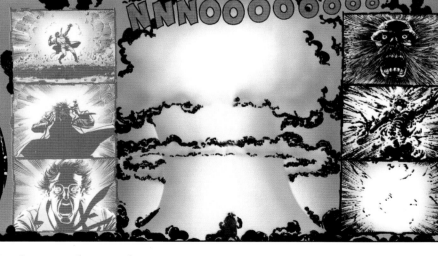

Back From the Dead

A few months after he returned to the present, Banner learned that the Maestro's spirit was still haunting the site of the first gamma-bomb test and might have been the reason why the Hulk always seemed able to return to that area. A large release of gamma radiation temporarily recreated the Maestro and allowed him to attack the Hulk. They battled until the Hulk managed to bury him beneath a few hundred tons of mountain debris.

Out of Her Time

The granddaughter of Rick Jones and Marlo Chandler, Janis was born in Dystopia and joined the rebel movement to overthrow the Maestro after her parents were slain by the Gravity Police. Trained in every martial art known in her time period, Janis wielded a quarterstaff that fired plasma bolts from either end. She convinced the other rebels to recruit the Hulk against the Maestro. Janis later used the time machine to rejoin the Hulk in the present.

WILD MAN

Alex Wildman was an average college student until the voices came. He discovered that he had the ability to take on one power from any superhuman. He could stretch his limbs like Mr. Fantastic or call upon a lightning bolt like Thor. He tried to capture Janis Jones, but the Hulk punched the voices right out of his mutant head.

TRAUMA™

HIS REAL NAME WAS TROH-MAW and he was heir
to a galactic empire. Born to Lord Armageddon, the
absolute monarch of an extraterrestrial race known as the
Troyjans, Trauma once had a twin. The two brothers never
liked each other and competed for their father's attention.
They both possessed superhuman strength and had the
ability to channel and expel cosmic energy. After studying
the arts of war and becoming experts at every form of
personal combat, they ravaged worlds and conquered
whole solar systems. The two brothers also journeyed to a
distant planet called Earth. They came to collect a family
debt, but one brother lost his life and the
other forfeited his heart.

AN ELIGIBLE ALIEN
*A hideous freak by human
standards, Trauma was
thought handsome by his fellow
Troyjans. He stood nearly
7 feet tall and weighed a little
over 1,000 lb. He was also a
little stronger than the Hulk.*

ALL FOR LOVE

Agamemnon, founder of the Pantheon, had promised the
Troyjans one of his descendants, and the two brothers
stormed the organization's headquarters. Atalanta slew
Trauma's twin while defending herself. Trauma often returned
to attack Atalanta, but she always managed to drive him
away. After the Hulk joined the Pantheon, Trauma cornered
Atalanta in the Himalayan Mountains and confessed his love
for her. He intended to take her back to his homeworld, but
the Hulk buried him beneath an avalanche.

*Targeted by special lenses
attached to his eyes, the
numerous weapons built
into his body armor were
triggered by his thoughts.*

The Troyjan War
Determined to make
Atalanta his bride, Trauma
returned to Earth and
kidnapped her. The Hulk
commandeered a spaceship
and led the Pantheon in hot
pursuit. Arriving on
Trauma's homeworld just in
time to stop the wedding,
the Hulk challenged the
Troyjan warrior to personal
combat. They battled until
Trauma stumbled over a
piece of shattered armor
and pierced his own heart.

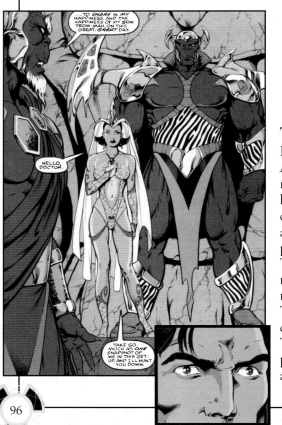

A DYING REQUEST
*Just before he died, Trauma proved he truly
loved Atalanta. He released the Pantheon
from their debt, and begged his father to grant
the Hulk and his friends safe passage to Earth.*

ARMAGEDDON™

I WANT *HIM* HERE. WE HAVE GONE TO TOO MUCH EFFORT, AND THE PRIZE IS TOO *IMPORTANT* TO ME.

I WANT MY WORTHY OPPONENT... FOR NONE LESS WILL DO.

THE TROYJAN EMPIRE was teetering on the brink of collapse when his father died in a space battle and Armageddon assumed the throne. Though only a teenager, the Troyjan warrior led his troops to victory after victory. Driven by an insatiable hunger to expand his power, Armageddon conquered many galaxies and ordered the slaughter of entire solar systems. He was so focused on his growing kingdom that he barely noticed when his wife died in childbirth after bearing him twin boys to carry on his bloodline. After entrusting their education to Lord Vittio, Armageddon forgot about his sons until one was killed on a mission to Earth. He was further outraged to discover that Trauma, his other son, was in love with his twin's murderer.

Target: the Hulk

Armageddon thought Trauma was an incompetent fool and only reluctantly gave him permission to wed Atalanta of the Pantheon. Armageddon didn't realize how much he loved his son until Trauma was accidentally killed while fighting the Hulk. Honor prevented the Troyjan monarch from immediately obliterating the Hulk, but he has hungered for vengeance ever since.

Armageddon can discharge beams of destructive force from his body.

THE RESURRECTION MACHINE

Though he promised not to harm the Hulk or the Pantheon, Armageddon was free to destroy Earth. He offered to exchange the planet's safety for the Hulk's help. The Troyjan Lord had learned that the Hulk's old enemy the Leader had built a machine that could revive the dead. Armageddon strapped the Hulk into the machine and attempted to transfer his life force into Trauma's body. But the green Goliath's personal power was too great and it incinerated the already dead Troyjan.

Lord Vittio

He barely stands 3 feet high, but Lord Vittio is one of the most powerful beings in the known universe. He is also Armageddon's most trusted friend and advisor. Like other members of the Troyjan race, Vittio can channel cosmic energy and may even be as deadly as the Silver Surfer.

PIECEMEAL ™

AMPHIBIOUS ANDROID
*Piecemeal is as much at home beneath the
ocean as on land. His tail propels him through
the water with the speed of a torpedo and his
body withstands the great pressures and freezing
temperatures that can occur under the sea.*

HE WAS CREATED in a secret laboratory in the Amazon jungle. Built to be
the ultimate killing machine, Piecemeal was assembled like the original
Frankenstein monster. Pieces of human and animal corpses were combined
with highly advanced weaponry to form the creature. The scientists who
constructed Piecemeal worked under the supervision of a would-be dictator
known as the Red Skull. Desiring a weapon that he could employ against any
superhuman foe, he planned to program Piecemeal's mind before sending the
creature out into the world. The Hulk became aware of the Skull's hidden
laboratory and attacked it, but Piecemeal escaped in the confusion. With his
mind still a blank slate, he wandered the jungle until he chanced upon a small
airport and stowed away on a cargo plane headed for Scotland.

*Battling Hulk, Piecemeal reveals
his ability to take on the powers
and appearance of his enemy.*

Created to Kill

Piecemeal can generate bursts
of bioelectricity from his
body and expel them with
sufficient force to shatter a
tank. His claws can shred
steel and his tail can crush a
concrete bunker. His most
amazing power, however, is
his ability to absorb the
memories and emotions of his
victims. He can also duplicate
their appearances and
superhuman powers.

THE NEW NESSIE

A retired member of the Pantheon who owned an inn on
Loch Ness sent for the Hulk when a new monster was
reported in the area. The Hulk learned that Piecemeal was
behind the sightings. The creature had been attacking tourists
and draining their minds. Piecemeal startled the Hulk by
assuming his appearance and duplicating some of his past
incarnations. Piecemeal is now believed to be dead, but
may still be living beneath the dark
waters of Loch Ness.

The Red Skull

The Red Skull is an international
terrorist who dreams of conquering
the world. A military and strategic
genius, he is a superb athlete and
master of all forms of hand-to-hand
combat. He is also a skilled
marksman and often employs his
"dust of death," which kills instantly
and causes the victim's skin to
shrivel and turn red so that the
corpse looks like it has a red skull.

> PROFESSOR...I'D HEARD YOU'D TAKEN ILL... BUT I WASN'T AWARE...

> THAT IT WAS THIS SERIOUS?

> I'VE TRIED NOT TO MAKE A BIG DEAL OF IT, BRUCE, OR LET TOO MANY PEOPLE KNOW.

DYING BY DEGREES
Crawford had contracted a degenerative nerve disease that was slowly paralyzing him. He grew weaker each day. Desperate to get well, he took advantage of his former student.

RAVAGE™

TRANSPORTED BY TELEPOD
Crawford's invention converted anything placed in one telepod into energy and transmitted it to a second telepod, where it was restored to its original form.

H E WAS THE TEACHER everyone wanted. Dr. Geoffrey Crawford, a physics professor at Desert State University took undergraduate Bruce Banner under his wing and became his mentor. Banner turned to his teacher for help after failing to find a cure for the Hulk. Crawford, by now a sick man, had invented a machine that could teleport matter. He realized that his device could be used to filter the gamma radiation from Banner's body. Crawford also came to believe that he could cure his own disease if he could obtain the Hulk's amazing recuperative powers. Crawford reconfigured his DNA to match Bruce's unique body chemistry and transformed himself into a Hulk-like monster called Ravage.

BETRAYED!

Ravage was bigger and slightly stronger than the Hulk. He also had Crawford's intellect and a hunger for personal power. He immediately tried to destroy the Hulk, but changed back into Crawford when the sun rose. Afraid that Banner would find a way to prevent him from becoming Ravage, Crawford betrayed his former student and turned him over to General Ross.

> STAND BY THAT FIRST POD, BRUCE.

> I JUST NEED TO TYPE SOME COMMANDS INTO THE COMPUTER...

> WHA--

> SHRAAK

Rescued by Ross

As the sun began to set, Crawford reentered the telepod and made the necessary adjustments so that he could remain in his Ravage form for the rest of his life. Finally free of his failing body and reveling in his new power, Ravage attacked the university and terrorized everyone who had ever pitied him. General Ross realized that only the Hulk could stop this new monster. Though he hated to do it, Ross freed his greatest enemy and sent him after Ravage. By working together, the Hulk and Ross managed to capture Ravage with a freezing ray.

THE DEATH OF BETTY BANNER

SHOCKING SYMPTOMS
Thinking she only had a simple rash, Betty was horrified when her body showed symptoms of massive cellular damage.

THEY LIVED AN EXTRAORDINARY life together, surviving everything from nuclear explosions to bizarre transformations and alien abductions. It seemed like they could survive everything except a happy ending. The Hulk possessed Banner's intelligence and had recently been granted a pardon by the U.S. President. After agreeing to work for the government, he was reunited with Betty and Rick Jones and given quarters in a secret base called Area 102, which was under the command of Colonel Cary St. Lawrence. For the first time since the accident that created the Hulk, Bruce Banner truly believed that he and Betty were finally going to get a chance to live happily ever after. His hopes were dashed after only a few hours when he suddenly heard Betty gasping for help. Her body was covered with open sores and she was obviously suffering from some form of radiation poisoning.

RACING THE CLOCK

With his wife dying in his arms, the Hulk smashed through whatever happened to be standing between him and the infirmary. He encased Betty within a special life-support unit and assembled the necessary medical team and equipment to save her. He knew that he only had a matter of hours to siphon off the radiation and stimulate new cellular growth in order to repair the damage to her body.

Her body covered in radiation lesions, Betty collapsed in Bruce's arms.

HIS WORST NIGHTMARE
When he learned that Betty's condition might have been caused by prolonged exposure to gamma radiation, Thunderbolt Ross threatened to kill Bruce Banner.

Desperate Gamble

Working against the clock, Banner modified a device that the military had build to drain radiation from the Hulk. He combined it with parts from the gamma ray machine he had used to control his transformations when he first became the Hulk. His aim was to try to get Betty to mimic the Hulk's regenerative powers before cleansing her body of radiation.

Only a genius like Bruce Banner could have conceived and cobbled together the amazing device that was used on his wife.

DESPITE BEST EFFORTS
With a silent prayer Bruce activated his machine. His spirits soared as Betty's skin started to regenerate. But something went wrong! Her heart failed and she died on May 9 at 10:39 a.m.

TOTAL DESPAIR
Bruce fell into a deep depression after his wife's funeral. He avoided his friends and locked himself in the old cave where he used to hide when he first became the Hulk. He had assumed that Betty's body had built up a natural tolerance for gamma radiation and couldn't believe that she was really gone.

FILLED WITH GUILT
The Hulk has never fully recovered from the loss of his wife. He is still haunted by her final moments and probably will be until the day he dies. He has only loved two women in his life—Betty and Jarella—and he cannot escape the fact that they both died because of him.

THE TRUE CULPRIT
Dr. Katherine Spar was sent to Area 102 by the Center For Disease Control to learn why Banner's gamma radiation had apparently killed Betty. After comparing blood samples, she discovered that Betty had been murdered—poisoned by the Abomination.

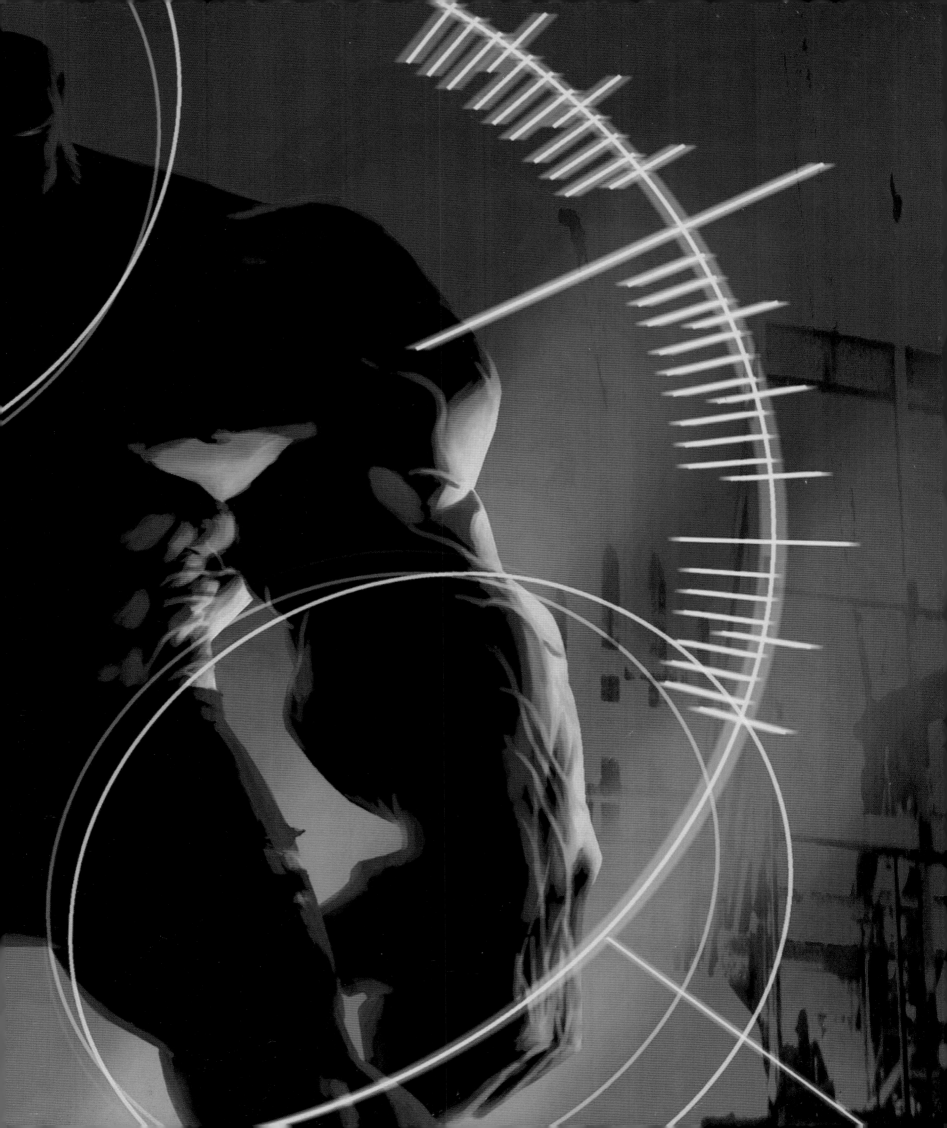

HULK IN THE 2000s

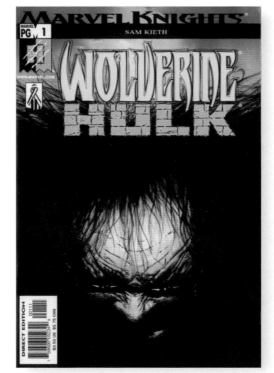

THE NEW MILLENNIUM had barely begun when *The Hulk* underwent a title change as *The Incredible* was reinstated to the masthead. After more than a 15-year absence, Sal Buscema returned to ink the series he had once penciled. Writer Paul Jenkins became artist Ron Garney's new partner and introduced the world to Dr. Angela Lipscombe, General John Riker, Gamma Dogs, and the Devil Hulk. Kyle Hotz was later tapped to handle the art chores and followed by illustrator John Romita, Jr. as Joe Fixit journeyed to Chicago to collect an old debt and the Hulk took final revenge on the Abomination. Bruce Banner was diagnosed with A.L.S. (Lou Gehrig's disease), and cured with the help of the Leader, his own dead father, and the creative team of Paul Jenkins, Sean McKeever, and Joe Bennett.

The original Defenders reunited and soon morphed into the Order, thanks to the creative efforts of Kurt Busiek, Erik Larson, Klaus Janson, Ron Frenz, Jo Duffy, and

Hulk Annual 2000: She-Hulk tries to help the Hulk mourn his deceased wife. (Painting by Mark Texiera)

Chris Batista. Writer Brian Azzarello and artist Richard Corben explored a guilt-haunted Hulk that might have been in *Startling Stories: Banner*, while Sam Keith reintroduced the Hulk to Wolverine for a four-issue series.

Novelist and screenwriter Bruce Jones now handled the scripting duties for the Hulk. Working with artists John Romita, Jr., Tom Palmer, Lee Weeks, Stuart Immonen, and Scott Kolish, Jones focused on Bruce Banner the man and returned the monster to the Hulk, filling the series with clandestine forces, relentless pursuit, deadly assassins, the walking dead, and more than a hint of horror.

Wolverine Hulk #1 (April 2002) : The mutant may get top billing, but we know who's the real star of this limited series. (Cover by Sam Keith)

The biggest news to Hulk fans was that a major motion picture was on the way. Produced by Universal Pictures and Marvel Entertainment, *Hulk* is directed by Ang Lee (best known for *Sense and Sensibility*, *The Ice Storm*, and *Crouching Tiger, Hidden Dragon*) and stars Eric Bana as Dr. Robert Bruce Banner, Jennifer Connelly as Elizabeth "Betty" Ross, and Sam Elliott as General Thaddeus "Thunderbolt" Ross. The film also features Nick Nolte as Dr. David Banner, Josh Lucas as Major Glen Talbot, and Lou Ferrigno (the Hulk in the classic 1970s television series) as the Head of Security.

2000

Hulk #12 (March 2000): Banner journeys into his subconscious with Joe Fixit and the mindless Hulk. (Cover by Ron Garney)

2001

Hulk # 25 (April 2001): Hulk gets his final revenge on the Abomination. (Cover by John Romita, Jr.)

2002

Hulk #40 (July 2002): The first appearance of Agent Pratt.(Cover by Kaare Andrews)

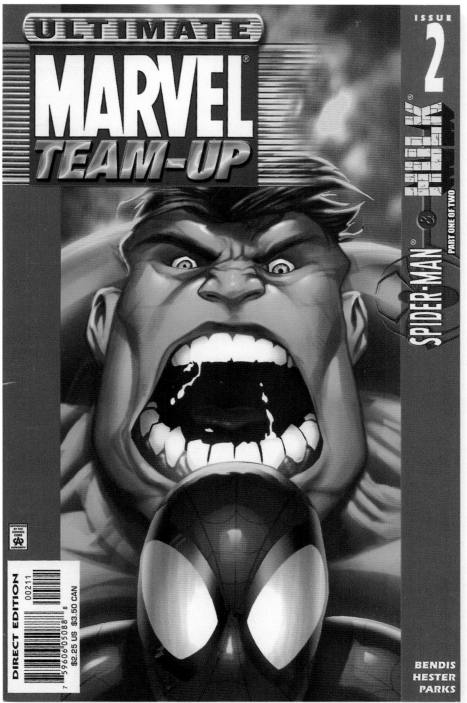

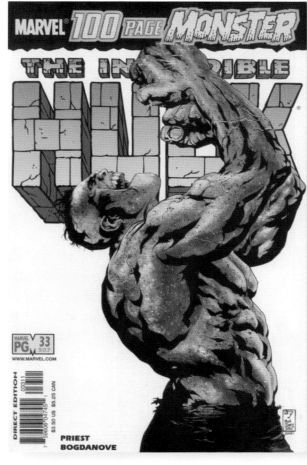

Hulk #33 *(Dec. 2001):*
The Hulk is betrayed by an old friend.
(Cover by J. H. Williams)

Ultimate Marvel Team-Up #2:
The first appearance of the Ultimate
Hulk (Cover by Phil Hester)

2002

Hulk #41 *(Aug.*
2002): The origin
of Lt. Sally Riker.
(Cover by Kaare
Andrews)

2002

The End of the
Hulk *(2002):*
Peter David reunites
with Dale Keown to
tell a final story.
(Cover by Dale
Keown)

2002

Hulk #42 *(Sept.*
2002): Agent Pratt
captures the Hulk.
(Cover by Kaare
Andrews)

GENERAL RYKER

GENERAL JOHN RYKER is a man who always gets what he wants. And what he wants is the Hulk. Secure in a top secret U.S. Army establishment equipped with state-of-the-art research facilities, with a battalion of troops armed with the latest in hi-tech weaponry, General Ryker plans to capture Bruce Banner and extract the secret of his radiation-derived power. His precise motives are known only to himself, but one thing is certain: this utterly ruthless military strategist will use any means and go to any lengths to achieve his objective. The lives of innocent people caught up in his web of cruelty and intrigue mean little or nothing to him.

Ryker's radiation experiments deformed Tibbetts' face and body.

HORRIFIC EXPERIMENTS
Hidden deep underground at Ryker's Groom Lake base is a lead-lined bunker. It is there that gruesome research into gamma radiation is carried out using kidnapped human beings as guinea pigs.

UGLY RUMORS
Ryker has several dark spots in his past. It is rumored that during the Vietnam War he deliberately dropped the toxic defoliant Agent Orange on US troops to study its effects. He may even have been involved in a U.S. President's assassination. He is an expert at brainwashing his men into obeying his commands.

THE DOGS OF WAR!

Locked away in his army stronghold, Ryker pushed his research team to go to any lengths to unlock the secrets of gamma radiation. His men scoured the hobo jungles of America's cities for tramps and vagrants to acts as human guinea pigs. One by one these "test subjects" died in agony—literally fried by their own nervous systems. In time Ryker realized that the key to creating his own Hulk lay in manipulating the subjects' minds. Suitable candidates were all around him—his own men!

Private Benjamin Tibbetts' strength is almost a match for the Hulk's—but not quite!

Ryker studied his men to find those most susceptible to mental manipulation.

HHAGHH!

ANGELA LIPSCOMBE

ANGELA LIPSCOMBE
Angela and Bruce were once close friends at medical school—very close friends. But when Angela achieved early success, Bruce was jealous and they drifted apart. Nevertheless Angela remained loyal to Bruce, and was keen to help him when he showed up at her home in obvious distress, believing he was afflicted with an incurable disease. Along with her lover, Doc Samson, Angela was later held hostage by Ryker, who was hoping to force the Hulk to give himself up.

The Hunt for the Hulk
Thanks to his vast intelligence network, Ryker soon tracked down Bruce Banner. He discovered that Banner was staying at the home of an old friend, psychologist Angela Lipscombe. The area was soon cordoned off and Ryker's troops moved in. However, at the last moment Banner mutated into the Gray Hulk called Joe Fixit. Snatching up Angela in his cupped hands, Joe Fixit made a successful bid for freedom across the rooftops—despite coming under fire from Ryker's battle tank.

Ryker's Secret
General Ross discovered that Ryker had a personal agenda for his cruel experiments into the effects of gamma radiation. He was trying to cure his wife, who was dying of cancer. She was horrified when she learned that innocent lives had been wasted in Ryker's attempt to save her life.

RYKER'S CREATURE
To combat Hulk's amazing physical strength, Ryker created his own gamma ray energized monster. He mutated one of his own men, Private Benjamin Tibbetts, into a deformed version of the Hulk, codename: Flux. To trigger Tibbetts' metamorphosis into a raging superbeast, Ryker made him believe that Dr. Banner had turned him into a monstrous freak. But the real causes of the soldier's mental turmoil lay deep within his own psyche.

I-I DON'T LIKE THIS NOW... I WANT MY...

...I WANT MY MOMMEE...

JINK SLATER

SOLO ACT
Jink Slater was a flamboyant assassin-for-hire who believed that he was the best in the business and preferred to work alone. It wasn't a question of money. Experience had taught him that few mercenaries could match his skills or courage and even fewer could be trusted.

JINK SLATER WAS a former Marine who was recruited by the C.I.A. after his discharge. After a brief and violent career as a covert operative, he decided to work for the bad guys because they paid better. Skilled in every form of personal combat, he served as the bodyguard for a Colombian drug lord and reputedly killed over eighteen drug enforcement agents. He later sold his services to a band of terrorists, who all died in a pipe bomb explosion, after attempting to renegotiate his fees. While training a paramilitary band in the Colorado Mountains, Slater was surrounded by the F.B.I. and only escaped by leaping across a fifteen-foot chasm. Slater was always up for a challenge and agreed to capture the Hulk for a secret cabal, but objected to being paired with Sandra Verdugo, another soldier of fortune.

Slater's gun fired a syringe-dart designed to lower the Hulk's blood pressure and render him unconscious.

Last Chance Café

The Hulk had been accused of murdering a young boy named Ricky Myers. Desperate to clear himself, Bruce Banner had shaved his head and was traveling across the country in disguise. Slater and Verdugo tracked the former scientist to the Last Chance Café where he was planning to meet Doc Samson. After entering the café, Samson recognized Slater and Verdugo and deliberately provoked Banner into transforming into the Hulk so that he could escape.

THE GAME
Slater was an army of one who killed without remorse. It was all a big game to him and he never thought he would lose.

TAG, YOU'RE DEAD

Convinced Verdugo had betrayed him, Slater shot her in the head and continued after the Hulk. Slater was an expert woodsman and easily picked up Banner's trail. He notified his mysterious employers that he intended to take the Hulk alone. They sent operatives to back him up, but Slater killed them because completing this mission had become a matter of personal pride. He tracked the Hulk to a cabin and found Verdugo still alive! Slater shot her again, but she got her revenge by detonating a bomb that apparently killed him.

SANDRA VERDUGO

SANDRA VERDUGO WAS ONE of the few women to become Airborne- and Ranger-qualified and serve with the Special Forces. She received advanced intelligence training and was recruited by the C.I.A., but chose to go private. An explosives and surveillance expert, she is a fine marksman and a martial arts master. She worked for anyone or any country that could meet her price. While running guns for an Argentine faction, she met an American businessman and had an affair. After the rebellion was put down, Verdugo fled the country without informing the father that she was pregnant. Eight years later, Verdugo was accused of murdering her own son and sentenced to death. While awaiting execution, she was approached by the same secret cabal that had hired Jink Slater and offered a chance to be reunited with her son.

LETHAL INJECTION
Verdugo was executed by lethal injection and pronounced dead. Her body was intercepted on its way to the morgue and subjected to a secret process known as H Section Programming.

Not even a bullet to the brain could kill Sandra Verdugo after she was programmed by H Section.

BACK FROM THE DEAD
Verdugo awoke in an empty room, seated before a television camera. Two voices informed her that it was now time to fulfill her part of the bargain. She was instructed to link up with Jink Slater and prove that she was a worthy partner. Posing as a maid, Verdugo sneaked into Slater's hotel and tried to get the drop on him. Slater preferred to work alone but realized that he might need help against the Hulk.

GIVE ME FIVE MORE MINUTES WITH HER!

YOU BOTH HAVE FIVE DAYS.

WHOEVER TAKES OUT BANNER FIRST GETS A BONUS.

YOU'RE A LIFE SAVER!

I'M SANDRA, MISTER...?

SMITH. BRUCE SMITH. WHAT CAN I GET YOU?

A Pleasant Distraction

Slater was the best assassin in the business, but Verdugo was a superior strategist and a master at misdirecting an enemy's attention at the right moment. When she spotted Banner at the Last Chance Café, she introduced herself and then drugged him with a spiked ring, which injected him with a powerful tranquilizer.

REVELATIONS

After the Hulk escaped the Café, Verdugo lured him to a cabin, where she revealed that Ricky Myers, the child he had allegedly killed, was her son. She claimed that the boy was still alive and a captive of the cabal that was after the Hulk. She also claimed that Doc Samson was the child's father. Though apparently killed in the same explosion that claimed the life of Jink Slater, Sandra later returned to help Banner clear his name and find her missing son.

LT. SALLY RIKER

SALLY RIKER GREW UP surrounded by cops. Her father, three brothers and most of her uncles were police officers. Riker studied criminal psychology in college and applied to the police academy against her father's wishes. She graduated near the top of her class and trained in hostage negotiation. After obtaining a masters degree in psychology, she was promoted to lieutenant and assigned her own team. She defused a number of hostage situations without losing a single life. Her record was spoiled when a criminal crew barricaded themselves inside a Denver bank and threatened to kill their hostages. Faced with taking out the gang's leader, Riker could not bring herself to take a life. She only wounded him and he killed a little girl before being subdued.

CRISIS OF CONFIDENCE
Blaming herself for the child's death and unable to bear being shunned by other cops, Riker resigned from the force, agreeing to remain on call until her replacement arrived. She even contemplated suicide, but resolved to battle on for those people who still depended on her, believing that a police officer had to set a good example.

BOILING POINT

Riker was called back into active duty when a former advertising executive reached a low point in his life and took the customers in a local convenience store hostage. Bruce Banner was in the store at the time and was chosen to serve as Riker's liaison with the gunman. To Riker's surprise, a group of men claiming to be F.B.I. agents soon arrived and took charge of the situation, but only seemed interested in Banner.

Shot in the chest by phony F.B.I. agents, Banner would have died if he hadn't turned into the Hulk.

Riker was an experienced negotiator and expert marksman, but even she wasn't prepared for the Hulk.

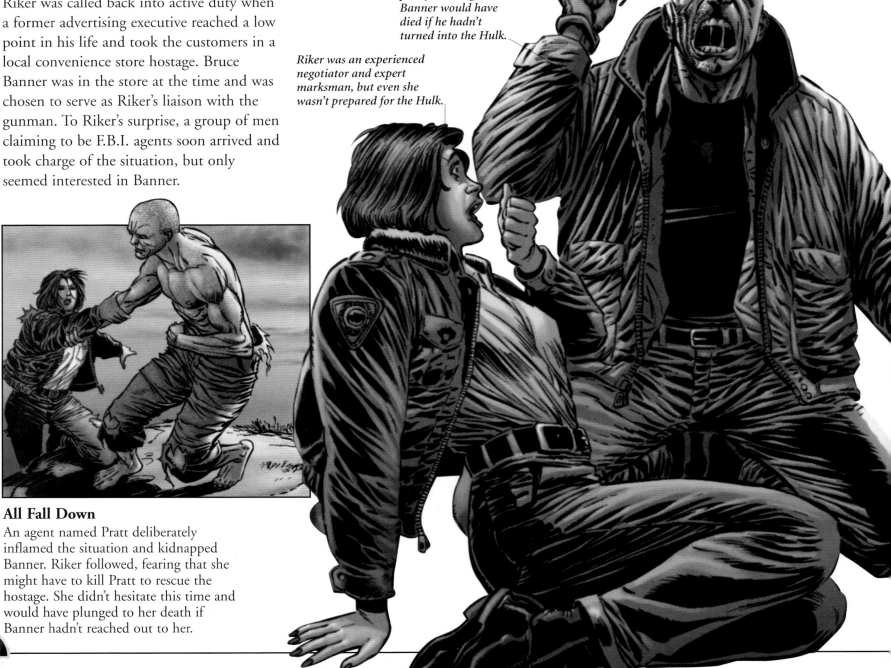

All Fall Down
An agent named Pratt deliberately inflamed the situation and kidnapped Banner. Riker followed, fearing that she might have to kill Pratt to rescue the hostage. She didn't hesitate this time and would have plunged to her death if Banner hadn't reached out to her.

AGENT PRATT

UTTERLY RUTHLESS
Pratt arrived in Miser with a sophisticated surveillance van and nearly a dozen men at his command, including a sniper. He had apparently been ordered to secure a sample of the Hulk's blood and ruthlessly endangered the entire town to achieve his goal. Pratt forced Banner to change into the Hulk, knowing full well that the monster would threaten lives and cause millions of dollars worth of damage.

SPECIAL AGENT
Pratt introduced himself as a Special Agent for the F.B.I., but Bruce Banner suspected he was an impostor.

VERY LITTLE IS KNOWN about the enigmatic Agent Pratt. He appears to work for the same clandestine organization that hired Jink Slater and Sandra Verdugo, but even that is questionable. Pratt entered the Hulk's life in a small town in Miser County, Colorado. Bruce Banner had been taken hostage in a convenience store. Pratt arrived on the scene and tried to get the local authorities to stand down. Without any regard for the safety of the other hostages, Pratt ordered his marksman to wound and traumatize Banner in order to draw out the Hulk. As soon as the Hulk emerged, Pratt sedated him with the same special syringe-dart gun that Jink Slater had once employed. After getting a sample of the Hulk's blood, Pratt murdered every member of his team and kidnapped the unconscious Banner.

Pratt habitually quotes from the poet Coleridge and the scientific genius Stephen Hawking.

His weapon of choice is a custom-made laser-scoped .22 with a built-in silencer

GROWING PAINS

As he tried to escape with Banner, Pratt revealed that he worked for a secret global organization that harbored the most advanced scientific minds and the deadliest operatives on the planet, but he may have been lying. Pratt was later injected with an artificial version of the Hulk's blood that caused acromegaly or gigantism. His body grew and grew, until his heart burst.

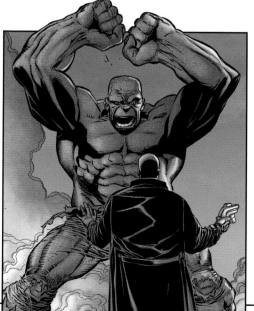

The Multiple Organism
After watching the man explode in front of him, Banner was convinced that he had seen the last of Agent Pratt. The former scientist realized that he was wrong a few weeks later when Pratt reentered his life. Having been subjected to H Section Programming, Pratt could revive from almost any wound and could even regrow missing limbs. Almost impossible to kill, Agent Pratt will never stop trying to capture the Hulk.

HULK 2099™

ULK 2099 LIVES in a future that may never come to pass. In this reality, multinational corporations rule the Earth. Eco-terrorists detonate the earthquake faults along eastern California in the year 2076, creating a great moat that separates the state from the mainland. Abandoned by the government, Los Angeles becomes a zone where the strong prey on the weak. John Eisenhart is a ruthless dealmaker for Lotusland Entertainment, but he gets a chance to become a hero when he discovers The Knights of the Banner, a cult devoted to Dr. Bruce Banner. When corporate assassins slaughter the Knights, John is exposed to gamma rays and becomes the Hulk of the year 2099.

Hero of the People
Haunted by his past misdeeds and the death of Gawain, the young friend who helped him become Hulk 2099, Eisenhart just wants to turn his back on civilization and head into the desert until he meets a young singer with a social conscience. Naomi Soon-Li Torrijos-Washington, who prefers to call herself Quirk, convinces him that he has a responsibility to become a hero of the people.

Hulk 2099 has razor-sharp fangs and claws that can tear steel.

LIVING ENGINE OF DESTRUCTION
Twelve feet tall and weighing 1,500 lb, Hulk 2099 can lift almost 150 tons and is practically indestructible. Although he possesses Eisenhart's intelligence, Hulk 2099 has an explosive temper and only feels alive when he's fighting

LET FREEDOM RING

Inspired by Quirk, Hulk 2099 leads his fellow wage-slaves in a revolt against the corporate monsters that control their lives and hunts down rogue scientists who are performing genetic experiments on the poor. He exposes religious charlatans and fights super-threats like Draco, Cybershaman, the Golden One, Vulx, Doom 2099 and the Anti-Hulk.

DEVIL HULK™

BRUCE BANNER'S personal demons appeared every time he thought of his father, especially when Doc Samson tried to psychoanalyze the Hulk. These monsters were other facets of his identity generated by his multiple personality disorder. With the aid of a machine built by Dr. Angela Lipscombe, Banner entered his own mind and found a cave full of thousands of Hulks. Furious at Banner's failure to protect his mother or Betty, a Guilt Hulk attacked his Savage Hulk and Joe Fixit personalities. As Banner continued to explore his subconscious, he discovered a Hulk that represented his darkest thoughts, a creature of unrelenting evil: his own Devil Hulk!

Snake Eyes

The Devil Hulk taunted Banner with a seductive whisper, claiming to be the only one strong enough to ignore all his guilt. The Devil Hulk was totally amoral, a creature of undiluted evil who swore that he would scratch his way to the surface of Banner's mind and take over his body.

Banner's sense of guilt threatened to overwhelm all his other personalities and release the Devil buried within his subconscious.

A Perfect World

Banner awoke one morning to discover that Betty was still alive and that they were the proud parents of two young daughters. He worked with his good friend Emil Blonsky and spent Saturdays fishing with his father or playing golf with his father-in-law. His life seemed perfect, but it began to unravel when he realized that it was just an illusion created by the Devil Hulk. Banner would have lived happily if he had only surrendered to the Devil.

EVE OF DESTRUCTION
The Gray and Savage Hulks have often teamed against the Devil. They know how much he hates the world. The Devil is far more vicious and dangerous than the Maestro and intends to leave the entire planet in ruins if he ever gets free.

THE ULTIMATES

ANOTHER VERSION OF the Hulk lives in an alternate universe. On this parallel Earth, government scientists created a super-soldier formula but it was lost when Captain America disappeared during World War II. Many years later, Bruce Banner was hired to recreate it. Working out of a rundown research facility in Pittsburgh, he engaged in secret superhuman trials on civilians and even tested the formula on himself. Instead of turning into a superhuman athlete, Banner became the Hulk and went on a cross-country rampage that climaxed in Manhattan when he battled the Ultimate Spider-Man. General Nick Fury took custody of Banner and hushed up his connection to Hulk. Fury needed Banner to complete his research in order to create a new super-team called the Ultimates.

THE TRISKELION
Located off the coast of Manhattan in upper New York Bay, the Triskelion is a 10-acre artificial island built to serve as the Ultimates' base. It contains living quarters, research labs and medical facilities, a superhuman containment center, a hydrobase, and an airplane hanger.

The Ultimate Spider-Man is a teenager named Peter Parker who possesses the proportionate strength, speed, and agility of a spider.

The Ultimate Hulk does not grow stronger as he gets angrier, and can only lift about 50 tons.

THE HULK TAKES MANHATTAN

Always the outsider, Banner did not get along with the other members of the team and his efforts to recreate the super-soldier serum only met with failure. His long romance with Betty Ross also hit a snag when she read a self-analysis book and decided that he was a toxic influence on her. Frustrated by his failures, he deliberately transformed into the Hulk and provided the Ultimates with their first super-menace.

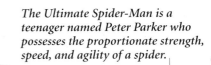

BEST LAID PLANS
General Fury had formed a personal bond with Bruce Banner and believed that he was the only one capable of recreating the original super-soldier serum.

ULTIMATE NICK FURY

General Fury answers directly to the U.S. President and heads a spying organization called S.H.I.E.L.D. Fury convinced his superiors to fund a $150 billion project to create a team of super-powered agents that could guarantee the planet's security.

Giant Man's maximum height is 60 ft; any higher and his skeleton could not support his body.

ULTIMATE GIANT MAN

Hank Pym is a cybertronics expert and a world authority on super-genetics. He used blood samples from his wife to create a formula that allowed him to grow to giant size. He also suffers from depression. Extremely jealous of his wife, Hank once almost killed her.

Ultimate Captain America

Steve Rogers was a scrawny runt who tried to enlist in the army when World War II broke out, but was unable to pass the physical. He volunteered to test the government's new super-soldier formula and was transformed into the ultimate warrior. Code-named Captain America, he disappeared while blowing up a Nazi lab in 1945. Found and revived only recently, Steve is still trying to adjust to the modern world.

Iron Man's helmet contains an interface that allows him to use his thoughts to control every operating system within his armor.

THE ULTIMATE WASP

Janet Van Dyne is a biologist married to Hank Pym. She is also a mutant who can grow wings and shrink to the size of a wasp. She eats caterpillars, hides in a larval nest whenever she is upset, and lays insect-like eggs every six weeks.

ULTIMATE THOR

The Norse god of thunder, Thor refused to answer Fury's calls because he didn't want to work for the military. He is an aggressive environmentalist who often appears in anti-corporate protests.

ULTIMATE IRON MAN

Tony Stark is an eccentric billionaire playboy with a trusted brand name in everything from Internet software to diet soda. He devised his Iron Man armor while climbing Mount Everest and joined the Ultimates after learning that he has an inoperable brain tumor.

THE END OF HULK

IN A FAR DISTANT FUTURE, which may or may not ever come to pass, a lone man limps across a barren landscape. A strange metal globe floats in the air, exactly 10 feet behind him. It is called a Vidot and it records every move he makes. The man's name is Bruce Banner and he is the last man on Earth. He knows this is true because he has spent over 100 years traveling the length and breadth of North America. He has seen only the occasional bird or animal, rotting vegetation, and plenty of cockroaches. Bruce pauses to crush one beneath his walking stick. He says his name aloud, just to remember what it sounds like. He has already forgotten so many sounds that he once took for granted. Too many years have passed since he last heard a car honk, a phone ring, or a baby cry. He sometimes visits the "Costumed Adventurers Memorial Park" where the remains of Spider-Man, Wolverine, and so many other super heroes have been laid to rest. After all their sacrifices to protect humanity, none could prevent the end of the world.

THE DAY THE EARTH DIED

It started with terrorists, escalated when governments retaliated, and eventually spiraled into nuclear holocaust. Millions of innocent people died when the bombs first fell. Billions more deaths followed as deadly radiation shrouded the entire planet. The Hulk didn't care. He managed to avoid being vaporized by the bombs and his body quickly healed any damage they did cause. The radiation just made him stronger. The Earth was dying, but that didn't bother the Hulk. He just wanted to be left alone.

GREEN SUNSET
Thanks to residual radiation left in the atmosphere after the Earth was devastated by war, the sky now turns green at sunset. But only Bruce Banner is left to admire this stunning vista.

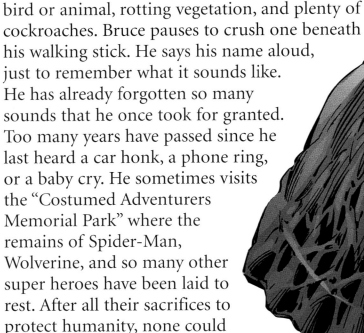

A HIDING PLACE
The noise of the explosions and the cries of the dying eventually did bother him. So the Hulk returned to New Mexico and sealed himself in the cave that he had once used as a base. Unable to move the massive boulder that blocked the exit, Banner was trapped inside as the months turned into years.

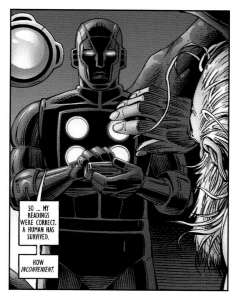

THE RECORDER
To Banner's surprise, the boulder was shoved aside one day by an alien robot named the Recorder who had been sent to document the demise of mankind. After informing Bruce that he was the last remaining human, the Recorder left the Vidot to chronicle his final days.

WASTING AWAY
Thanks to the Hulk's immunity to radiation, recuperative powers, and ability to eat almost anything, Banner lived far beyond a normal life span. He eventually lost all track of time and came to believe he was over 200 years old.

ANGRY AND ALONE
Coming out only at night or when Banner grew agitated, the Hulk missed no one. He reveled in the fact that his enemies were no more, that everyone who ever feared or tried to hurt him was dead. Everyone except Banner and the bugs! The Hulk could feel the puny scientist rattling around in his head. More than the Leader, more than the Abomination, the Hulk had always hated Banner and still dreamed of being free of him, but the cockroaches were the real problem...

ONLY THE BUGS REMAIN
Scientists had long theorized that only the cockroach could survive and adapt after a nuclear war. The theory became a terrifying reality when vast swarms of these insects inherited the planet. They often attacked the Hulk, trying to consume him, but his uncanny healing ability kept him alive.

THE WAR IS OVER
The war between Bruce Banner and the incredible Hulk did not conclude until the former scientist took his last breath.

Hollow Victory
The Hulk could survive almost any catastrophe. Banner, however, was only human. Though he had somehow stayed alive for more than 200 years, his body was finally running down. He awoke one night, feeling as if his chest was on fire, and knew that his suffering was almost over. Fighting like a caged animal, the green Goliath broke free, refusing to surrender to death. The Hulk realized at once that something was different. Bruce Banner was dead. Knowing that he, too, would die if he ever changed back into human form, the Hulk sat and waited. He had always wanted to be alone… and he had finally gotten his wish.

HULK AROUND THE WORLD

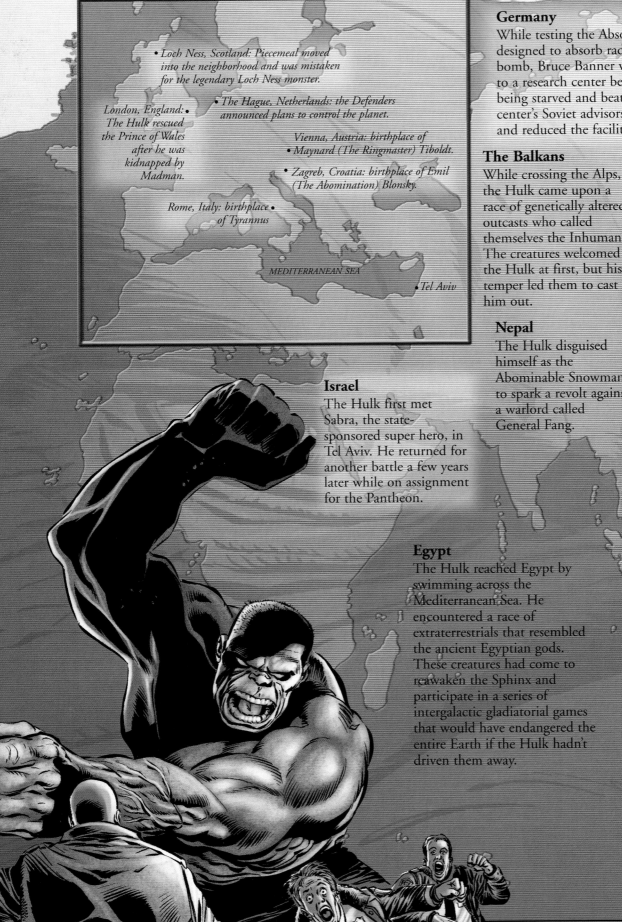

- Loch Ness, Scotland: Piecemeal moved into the neighborhood and was mistaken for the legendary Loch Ness monster.

London, England: The Hulk rescued the Prince of Wales after he was kidnapped by Madman.

- The Hague, Netherlands: the Defenders announced plans to control the planet.

Vienna, Austria: birthplace of • Maynard (The Ringmaster) Tiboldt.

- Zagreb, Croatia: birthplace of Emil (The Abomination) Blonsky.

Rome, Italy: birthplace • of Tyrannus

MEDITERRANEAN SEA

• Tel Aviv

Germany
While testing the Absorbatron, an invention designed to absorb radiation from an atomic bomb, Bruce Banner was kidnapped and smuggled to a research center behind the Iron Curtain. After being starved and beaten for refusing to help the center's Soviet advisors, Banner became the Hulk and reduced the facility to rubble.

The Balkans
While crossing the Alps, the Hulk came upon a race of genetically altered outcasts who called themselves the Inhumans. The creatures welcomed the Hulk at first, but his temper led them to cast him out.

Mongolia
After being stranded by the Hulk, Bruce Banner was captured by hill bandit Kang Khan who tried to ransom him back to the United States.

Nepal
The Hulk disguised himself as the Abominable Snowman to spark a revolt against a warlord called General Fang.

Republic of China
After teleporting the Hulk to his castle in the northern mountains, a would-be dictator called the Mandarin placed a device on the monster's neck and took over his mind. The Mandarin planned to topple the Communist regime before sending the Hulk against the U.S. Nick Fury and his S.H.I.E.L.D. agents stormed the castle and helped the Hulk escape.

Israel
The Hulk first met Sabra, the state-sponsored super hero, in Tel Aviv. He returned for another battle a few years later while on assignment for the Pantheon.

Egypt
The Hulk reached Egypt by swimming across the Mediterranean Sea. He encountered a race of extraterrestrials that resembled the ancient Egyptian gods. These creatures had come to reawaken the Sphinx and participate in a series of intergalactic gladiatorial games that would have endangered the entire Earth if the Hulk hadn't driven them away.

NORTHERN TERRITORY

• Alice Springs

Australia
Born in Alice Springs in the Northern Territory, Fred (Boomerang) Myers trained for many hours each day until he achieved absolute control over his signature weapon.

Arctic circle

Location of Bitterfrost, the secret underground headquarters where the Gremlin imprisoned the real Glenn Talbot while an imposter was sent to the U.S. to assassinate the President.

Seattle, Washington: Possessing Banner's intelligence, the Hulk worked at Northwind Laboratory, hiring Dr. Kate Waynesboro as his research assistant.

Boise, Idaho: birthplace of Samuel (The Leader) Sterns and Philip (Madman) Sterns.

Buffalo, New York: the Hulk journeyed to Niagara Falls to stop Betty Ross marrying Major Glenn Talbot, but got distracted when he encountered Tiger Shark.

Dayton, Ohio: birthplace of Bruce Banner.

Las Vegas, Nevada: the site of the Coliseum hotel and casino that employed Joe Fixit.

Los Angeles, California: birthplace of Jennifer (She-Hulk) Walters.

Plunketville, Florida: Using the Hulk as bait, Xemnu tried to kill the other Defenders.

Desert Base, New Mexico: site of the gamma bomb test that created the Hulk.

Florida Everglades: where the Hulk met the Glob.

Canada

During his many cross-country travels across the U.S., the Hulk has made many side trips into Canada. He first encountered the Wendigo and Wolverine in the Canadian north woods. The Leader established Freehold beneath the ice fields near Alberta and the Hulk had his first battle with Doctor Walter (Sasquatch) Langkowski in British Columbia.

Florida

The Pantheon sends the Hulk to find Dr. Sumner Beckwith, one of their researchers who has also disappeared. The Hulk learns that the scientist has been using gene mutation in an attempt to recreate Captain America's super-soldier formula and has accidentally transformed himself into a mindless swamp monster.

Easter Island

After swimming in the Pacific Ocean for several days, the Hulk was nearly exhausted when he crawled ashore at Easter Island. He collapsed on the beach and transformed back into Bruce Banner. Crusher (the Absorbing Man) Creel had also sought the island's safety and soon took the unconscious Banner prisoner. In the battle that followed Creel accidentally became a small island.

Central America

Seeking a quiet place to rest, Bruce Banner wandered into the town of Costa Salvador where he learned that an Inhuman named Maximus the Magnificent had used a giant robot to enslave the population. Maximus misguidedly tried to recruit the Hulk in his bid for world conquest.

Brazil

Sent to the Amazon jungle by the Pantheon, the Hulk was captured and brainwashed by the Red Skull who paired him with the Juggernaut and sent them to battle the Avengers. Forced to relive some painful memories of his father, the Hulk regained his senses and destroyed the Red Skull's base, which included the laboratory that had constructed Piecemeal.

Costa Salvador

The Savage Land

This tropical land that time forgot is located in Antarctica. The Hulk happened to find himself there and discovered that an alien invader was planning to use a weather-making machine to cleanse the Earth of humanity.

The Savage Land

GAZETTEER

CHARACTER	FIRST APPEARANCE
Abomination (Emil Blonsky)	TTA #80
Abominatrix	SH2 #21
Absorbing Man (Carl "Crusher" Creel)	JIM #114
Achilles	H2 #379
Agamemnon	H2 #381
Ajax	H2 #379
Alpha Flight	XM #120
Ant-Man (Dr. Henry Pym)	TTA #27
Apocalypse	XF #5
Arabian Knight (Abdul Qamar)	H2 #257
Armageddon	H2 #413
Armbruster, Colonel John	H2 #164
Atalanta	H2 #379
Augustus, Romulus (Tyrannus)	H1 #5
Avengers	AV #1
Baker, William (Sandman)	ASM #4
Banner, Betty (a.k.a. Betty Ross)	H1 #1
Banner, Brian	H2 #312
Banner, Dr. Robert Bruce	H1 #1
Banner, Rebecca	H2 #312
Bat-Seraph Ruth (Sabra)	H2 #256
Bereet	RHM #1
Berengetti, Michael	H2 #347
Bi-Beast	H2 #169
Boomerang (Fred Myers)	TTA #81
Blonsky, Emil (The Abomination)	TTA #90
Bruto, the Strongman	H1 #3
Captain America	CA #1
Captain Marvel (Genis-Vell)	SSA #6
Chandler, Marlo (a.k.a. Marlo Chandler-Jones)	H2 #347
Circus Of Crime	H1 #3
Clown (Eliot "Crafty" Franklin)	H1 #3
Crawford, Dr. Geoffrey (Ravage)	RHC #2
Creel, Crusher	JIM #114
Crimson Dynamo	TOS #46
Dark-Crawler	H2 #126
Darkstar (Laynia Petrovna)	CH #7
Darnell, Ann (Vapor)	H2 #254
Darnell, Jimmy (X-Ray)	H2 #254
Dornova, Nadia (wife of Emil Blonsky)	H2 #382
Drenkov, Igor (Igor Starsky)	H1 #1
DuBois, Zelda (Princess Python)	ASM #22
Eisenhart, John (Hulk 2099)	TU #1
Fantastic Four	FF #1
Flux (Private Benjamin Tibbetts)	H3 #17
Franklin, Eliot (The Clown)	H1 #3
Fury, Nick	SGF #1
Galaxy Master	H2 #111
Gambonno, Ernesto	ASM #16
Gambonno, Luigi	ASM #16
Genis-Vell (Captain Marvel)	SSA #6
Glob	H2 #121
Glorian	H2 #190
Gremlin	H2 #163
Grimm, Benjamin J. (the Thing)	FF #1
Gyrich, Henry Peter	AV #168
Halflife (Tony Masterson)	H2 #334
Harrison, Jessie (Jailbait)	H2 #345
Horowitz, Burt (Omnibus)	H2 #345
Hotshot (Lou Stewart)	H2 #366
Hulk (Dr. Robert Bruce Banner)	H1 #1
Hulk 2099 (John Eisenhart)	TU #1
Hulkbusters	H2 #317
Human Cannonball (Jack Pulver)	H1 #3
Human Torch (Johnny Storm)	FF #1
Invisible Woman (Susan Richards)	FF #1
Ironclad (Mike Steel)	H2 #254
Iron Man (Tony Stark)	TOS #39
Jackson, Crackerjack	H2 #182
Jacobson, Susan	H2 #226
Jailbait (Jessie Harrison)	H2 #366
Jarella	H2 #140
Jones, Janis	FI #1
Jones, Rick	H1 #1
Juggernaut (Cain Marko)	XM #12
Khan, Kang	TTA #67
Krylenko, Nikolai (Vanguard)	IM #109
Langkowski, Dr. Walter	XM #120
LaRoquette, Samuel J. (Rock)	H2 #317
Leader (Samuel Sterns)	TTA #62
Lipscombe, Dr. Angela	H3 #12
Loki	JIM #55
Lord Visis	H2 #140
MacPherran, Mary (Titania)	SW #3
Madman (Phil Sterns)	H2 #364
Maestro	FI #1
Marko, Cain (Juggernaut)	XM #12
Martel, Dr. Armand	H2 #317
Masterson, Tony (Halflife)	H2 #334

AFTERWORD

BRUCE BANNER IS SOMEONE we all know. He is everyone with a secret, every child afraid of the monster under the bed and every adult who ever dared a glimpse at his own inner beast. He's both the bully in the schoolyard and the victim cowering on the ground. He is us.

I first met the Hulk when I was 11 years old, a golden age for any comic book fan. Already a devotee of Stan Lee and Jack Kirby and their work on *The Fantastic Four*, I couldn't wait to read their newest creation. To be honest, I was a little disappointed with the first issue. It didn't seem to have the heart or humor of the aforementioned FF, but there was something about the character that struck a nerve. As the oldest of seven children, I could easily identify with a someone who had to control his temper. I bought all six issues of *The Incredible Hulk* and was downright angry when the title ceased publication. I was pleased when old greenskin appeared in *The Avengers #1* and was positively blown away when he battled the blue-eyed Thing in *Fantastic Four #25*, the first comic book that ever truly defined heroism for me.

Whenever I think of the Hulk, seven people immediately spring to mind. I think of Stan Lee and Jack Kirby who created the character and Len Wein whose interpretation of the Hulk really sparked my imagination. Herb Trimpe and Sal Buscema, two good friends and great artists that I have been privileged to work with over the years, still define old greenskin to me. I have to confess that my favorite Hulk author was, and probably always will be, Peter David whose insight, creativity, craft, and tenderness for the character blueprints the way to write a monthly comic book series. I must also mention Bobbie Chase, who served as Peter's editor, advocate and safety net for most of his run. She always seemed to know when to let him run wild and when to apply the brakes.

The time has come to thank my own editor, Alastair Dougall, for his patience and guidance. I am also grateful to Daniel Bunyan who designed this book and blew me away with one stunning layout after another. I also owe Mark Beazley for suggesting me for this project.

While the original comics were my actual source material, I also relied rather heavily on the work of people like Mark Gruenwald, Peter Sanderson, Elliot Brown, Mark Bernardo, Bob Budiansky, Tom Brevoort, Eric Fein and all the others who contributed to The Official Handbook Of The Marvel Universe (all three editions). The Internet has also become an amazing source of information and Hulk fans will enjoy a visit to Incrediblehulk.com, leaderslair.crosswinds.net or comicboards.com.

Anyone interested in old greenskin should also look in on the monthly comic book because Bruce Jones and company are doing some very fine work. The Hulk's earlier adventures have been reprinted in a variety of formats, from the pricey *Marvel Masterworks* to the economical *Essential* editions and dozens of trade paperbacks. I also give Peter David's Hulk novel *What Savage Beast* my highest recommendation.

This book is dedicated to the ever-patient Patricia E. who didn't even blink when she returned home one day to find every available surface in the kitchen, living and dining rooms covered with Hulk comics. And I must also acknowledge Jimmy, Bernie, Danielle, Tommy, Christopher, Allison, Stephen, Meredith, Alexa, Andrew, Gerald and Carolyn who often give their grouchy old uncle a reason to remain a storyteller. I would also like to express my gratitude to you, my reader, for just being there!

HOO-HA!

Tom D.

INDEX

Main entries are in **bold**.

ACKNOWLEDGMENTS

Dorling Kinderseley would like to thank the following people:

Seth Lehman and Mark Beazley at Marvel Enterprises, Inc.

Stan Lee for the Foreword.

Hilary Bird for the Index.

Julia March and Mary Atkinson for editorial assistance.